MAKERS
of the
MUSLIM
WORLD

Ikhwan al-Safa'

"Its style is eloquent and lucid, and its arguments are coherent and delicately articulated. The author shows clear signs of scholarly expertise in the field, combined with exegetical rigour and hermeneutic sensitivity in interpretation. The text is informative and its reading is enjoyable as well as engaging."

DR NADER EL-BIZRI, THE INSTITUTE OF ISMAILI STUDIES

SELECTION OF TITLES IN THE MAKERS OF THE MUSLIM WORLD SERIES

Series editor: Patricia Crone,
Institute for Advanced Study, Princeton

'Abd al-Malik, Chase F. Robinson
Abd al-Rahman III, Maribel Fierro
Abu Nuwas, Philip Kennedy
Ahmad ibn Hanbal, Christopher Melchert
Ahmad Riza Khan Barelwi, Usha Sanyal
Al-Ma'mun, Michael Cooperson
Al-Mutanabbi, Margaret Larkin
Amir Khusraw, Sunil Sharma
Beshir Agha, Jane Hathaway
Fazlallah Astarabadi and the Hurufis, Shazad Bashir
Ibn 'Arabi, William C. Chittick
Ibn Fudi, Ahmad Dallal
Ikhwan al-Safa', Godefroid de Callataÿ
Shaykh Mufid, Tamima Bayhom-Daou

For current information and details of other books in the series, please visit www.oneworld-publications.com/subjects/makers-of-muslim-world.htm

MAKERS
of the
MUSLIM
WORLD

Ikhwan al-Safa'

A Brotherhood of Idealists on the Fringe of Orthodox Islam

GODEFROID DE CALLATAŸ

ONEWORLD
ACADEMIC

A Oneworld Academic Book

First published by Oneworld Publications, 2005
Reprinted, 2017, 2020

A CIP record for this title is available from the British Library

ISBN 978-1-85168-404-5
eISBN 978-1-78074-196-3

Typeset by Sparks, Oxford, UK
Cover and text design by Design Deluxe
Printed and bound in Great Britain by Clays Ltd, Elcograf S.p.A.

Oneworld Publications
10 Bloomsbury Street
London WC1B 3SR

CONTENTS

ACKNOWLEDGEMENT

The first and greatest debt I owe is, of course, to Patricia Crone. Not only did Patricia offer me the opportunity to write a book in the Makers of the Muslim World series, she also spent a tremendous amount of time and energy to supervise it at every stage of its making. I am grateful to Charles Burnett and Nader el-Bizri, for many valuable comments and suggestions on various points of the discussion. I also wish to express my gratitude to Oneworld Publications, for the excellent work they have done on my manuscript. Finally, I have much pleasure in thanking Paula Lorente Fernández for her unfailing trust, constant assistance, and loving encouragement throughout. Este libro está dedicado a ella y a Gabriela, nuestra hija recién nacida, con quien tantas cosas tendremos que aprender.

INTRODUCTION

This book is concerned with a collection of around fifty epistles published anonymously in Iraq in the tenth century by people who called themselves the Brethren of Purity (*Ikhwan al-Safa'*). Exactly who they were is disputed. Most probably they were secretaries from the local bureaucracy in Basra, a city in southern Iraq, but not everyone agrees. Whoever they were, it is not possible to write a biography of any one of them, or of all of them together. If they have been included in this series even so, it is because one can still produce a spiritual portrait of them. Their work puts forward a coherent intellectual system, a view of the world that many deemed to be heretical, but which none the less never ceased to find readers over the centuries. The influence of the Brethren, albeit not often publicly acknowledged, on many great figures of Islamic thinking was considerable. The Epistles (*Rasa'il*) of the Brethren of Purity, as the work is usually referred to, survive to this day in a great number of manuscripts.

There are two reasons why the Epistles were unacceptable to most Sunni Muslims (who constituted the majority then as now). First, they were clearly Shi'ite in nature, and second, they were patently philosophical, more precisely Neoplatonist or, as the great theologian Ghazali (d. 1111) would have it, Pythagorean. They were in fact a characteristic product of the tenth century, a period of extraordinary intellectual activity in the Muslim world. In the rest of this Introduction I shall say more about these three features.

SHI'ISM

Shi'ism originated in a disagreement over the succession to the caliphate. All Shi'ites hold that only members of the Prophet's family were qualified for the leadership of the Muslim community, known as the imamate or, almost synonymously, the caliphate. The disagreement soon broadened to include different views of the imam's functions. The Shi'ites saw him as much more of a religious guide than did other Muslims, claiming that one could not achieve salvation without him since he alone had the faculty of understanding the secret meaning of the Revelation. By the tenth century the Shi'ites had divided into four main groups.

The most important, numerically speaking, was Imami Shi'ism, which believed that a succession of twelve imams had led the devotees from the Prophet's time until 874, when the twelfth went into hiding. Waiting for his reappearance as a messiah at the end of time, and simultaneously exalting the martyrs of the past, the Imami Shi'ites soon abandoned any hope of playing a political role. But as a depoliticized creed it was attractive to the various rulers who followed the break-up of the caliphate. The Abbasids, who had previously dominated most of the Muslim world and who had represented Sunni orthodoxy up to that time, were from now on powerless. Since 945, they had fallen under the control of the Buyids, Iranian mercenaries from the Caspian coast who had established themselves in Iraq and western Iran. They patronized Imamism after their arrival in Iraq. The Hamdanids, a minor dynasty in Syria, were also Shi'ite, probably Imami as well.

The second type of Shi'ism was Zaydism, a more militant form, which by the tenth century had managed to occupy Yemen and Daylam. The Buyids had probably professed Zaydism before their arrival in Iraq. The third type was made up of extremists of various kinds, whose range of beliefs generally included such "exaggerated" convictions as the transmigration of souls or the assimilation of such or such imam to divinity.

And the fourth was Ismailism, which had grown from Imami and extremist roots, to emerge in full towards the end of the ninth century. Ismailism was a complex set of religious, social, and intellectual doctrines, whose purpose was to offer a unified and global theory about God, the world, and the place of humankind in history. Like Imamis, Ismailis exalted their martyrs as well as their own lineage of seven imams – the last of whom had disappeared in the second half of the eighth century. But Ismailism distinguished itself by promoting a particularly elaborate doctrine about the division of world history, which it divided into seven cycles, each allegedly heralded by a prophet. Unlike Imamism, it was also a virulently political branch of Shi'ism which made remarkably efficient use of both military force and propaganda. One may recall here the many troubles caused in Iraq and the Gulf by a group of Ismaili revolutionaries known as Qarmatis, who on one occasion even succeeded in stealing the Black Stone from Mecca. But the greatest triumph of Ismailism occurred when another group, which had earlier appeared in Tunisia, took control of Egypt in 969. They were the Fatimids, who were powerful enough to claim the supreme title of the caliphate for themselves. In all, Shi'ism was clearly gaining ground in the tenth century, in spite of its inner divisions. The Sunnis, though numerically the majority, were forced to share power in many places.

It has often been assumed that the Brethren of Purity were Ismailis. But this is clearly more problematic than their general affiliation to Shi'ism. For while the Epistles do have much in common with Ismaili tenets, it also seems impossible to link the authors with any historical faction of Ismailism that we know about. The present essay will add a few elements to discussion without providing any definitive answer. This does not mean that I view the problem as trifling. I am convinced that the corpus of epistles should be looked at with the least possible degree of prejudice, and that regarding it simply as a pure product of Ismailism (as various scholars have done in the past) inevitably has an adverse effect on one's interpretation. Besides, as should become increasingly clear in the course of the discussion, it seems to me that so restrictive a definition is in itself incompatible with the very eclecticism shown by the Brethren throughout their work.

PHILOSOPHY

Before the rise of Islam, the Near East had already served as a center in which philosophy, or in other words the whole corpus of rational wisdom inherited from antiquity, continued to be cultivated as it receded from the western Mediterranean. Communities of philosophers, mostly but not exclusively Christians, were found in cities such as Mosul, Edessa, Jundishapur, and Harran. A rich tradition was maintained in Greek, Syriac, and Persian, a tradition which continued to develop even after the sudden arrival of the Arabs. The irruption of Islam and, as early as the beginning of the eighth century, its rapid expansion as far as Spain and India, did not at first fundamentally affect this order of things. Towards the end of the Umayyad caliphate (750 CE), however, and especially under the first Abbasids, there began an unprecedented movement to translate this tradition into Arabic, the new ruling language. This formidable undertaking would not be over before the end of the tenth century when, with the exception of a limited amount of specific literature not deemed by the scholars of Islam to be of interest, nearly all Greek sources accessible in that part of the world seem to have been made available in the Arabic language. The breadth of the field, which ranges from logic and metaphysics to ethics and politics, from medicine and the natural sciences to the sciences of number (arithmetic, geometry, music, and astronomy), and the technical sciences, is impressive. There was an unusually rich melting pot of cultures, races, and religions in which diverse groups of translators, copyists, and scientists were able to work with one another for more than two centuries. Much of their work was commissioned by the caliphs, especially in the beginning, but there was no single sponsor and no centralized program. This makes their achievement all the more impressive. Among the translators, Christians, once again, were in the majority, but there were also Jews, Persians, Arabs, and even idolaters, for pagans still survived in the city of Harran, where a cult of planetary divinities continued until at least the tenth century. Needless to say, this multiculturalism was also to favor significantly the incorporation of sources that did not ultimately derive from Greece, but rather from India, Iran, and ancient Mesopotamia.

Philosophy and the rest of rational sciences did not easily find their place in the already well-structured building of Islamic thinking. At the moment when they finally made their appearance, the field of theoretic knowledge was still largely the prerogative of traditional sciences, in other words sciences which, like jurisprudence (*fiqh*) and theology (*kalam*), could be viewed as grounded in the Qur'an and the traditions of the Prophet. A certain evolution was perceptible, though. Prompted, as it were, by its own queries, Islamic theology slowly began to open itself to the outcome of independent reasoning. Mu'tazilism, a school of theologians with avowed rationalist bias, became very influential. For some time in the first half of the ninth century, it even received the support of the caliphs in Baghdad, then at the height of their power. It is no accident that the great figure of Kindi (d. c. 870) came into view in that period, too. Kindi, closely involved in the translation movement of works from classical antiquity, was the first among the great philosophers writing in Arabic. As such, he and his circle went down in history as the first thinkers to try to harmonize the pagan heritage of Greece with the divine truth revealed in the sacred text of Islam and the life of Muhammad. Kindi's monumental work, of which only a fraction has survived, bears witness to the fact that he was much more a polymath than a philosopher in the narrow sense. He wrote on nearly all topics, from mathematics to physics, from history to magic. What is also apparent in his treatises is that among the various philosophers of antiquity he had the greatest admiration for Plato and Aristotle (both fourth century BCE). This was true of most philosophers in the tenth century. But in his case as later, one of the two masters tended to have the preponderant influence, so that it is customary to distinguish between Aristotelians and Platonists.

The Brethren of Purity are clearly to be ranged among those who were mostly influenced by Platonist, or more exactly Neoplatonist, philosophy. Indeed, for a substantial part, their way of thinking is closely reminiscent of certain theoretic constructions elaborated in late antiquity by Neoplatonists such as Plotinus (third century CE) or Proclus (fifth century CE). Like them, the Brethren made much of the idea that man is a sort of world in miniature, for example. Similarly, they held that the world was set in motion by the World Soul, and that among individual souls only those of true philosophers would be able to rise again to their divine origin. To a certain extent, one could even say that the Brethren went further than their Greek predecessors in their syncretism, which had been a notable feature of Neoplatonism in antiquity. All this is true, but it seems to me that there is some risk, if not some mistake, in reducing the Brethren's philosophical conceptions to that dimension alone. The present essay will hopefully make this clear, especially when it comes to investigate the use the Brethren made of their sources.

THE TENTH CENTURY

At first sight, the Islamic world in the tenth century seems a paradoxical phenomenon. On the one hand, it was characterized by a striking political instability, of which the almost complete collapse of the caliphate is the most obvious example. On the other hand, it was also characterized by an intellectual effervescence and a cultural dynamism of a rare intensity – so much so that it is portrayed as a kind of golden age of Arab-Muslim thinking in many history textbooks, which usually illustrate this splendor by lining up the big names of the time: the philosophers Farabi and Miskawayh, the poet Mutanabbi, the historian Mas'udi, the geographer Maqdisi, the astronomer Sufi, or the mystic Hallaj. In fact, the paradox we have to cope with is not as real as it seems. The decentralization of power may well have played a very positive role in the process. First, it most probably favored the resurgence of many local traditions, whether of an ethnic or a religious nature, which had for some time been dimmed by the Arab conquests. Second, it certainly contributed to the availability of patronage, as newly arrived rulers competed with each other to take the place of the Abbasid caliphs as protectors of the arts and sciences. Among these dynasties which became famous for their patronage of artists and scholars of all kinds one finds, in addition to the Sunni Umayyads in Spain, the names of several Shi'ite ruling families such as the Buyids in Iraq, the Hamdanids in Syria, and the Fatimids in Egypt.

Amid the vast array of works produced during this golden age of Muslim literature in Arabic, the Epistles of the Brethren of Purity clearly stand out as a strange and unusual work, yet a work which reflects its own time as very few other contemporaneous creations do. For the authors conceived it as a sort of all-encompassing encyclopaedia of human knowledge, and this necessarily means that they had to acquaint themselves with both the historical background and the current debates in each of the disciplines they treated. A substantial part of the present book has been dedicated to the encyclopaedic nature of the Brethren's project, since this obviously makes them unique in the history of Arabic literature and probably also in the history of literature *tout court*. It has seemed convenient to arrange this essay in six chapters, each illustrating a particular facet of our topic.

- Chapter 1, "Esotericism," provides a general overview. It highlights, above all, the striking contrast between the anonymous authors, whose greatest exploit must be to have managed to conceal their identity up to the present day, and their relatively well-defined corpus of texts which seems to have been passed down over the centuries without any notable changes.
- Chapter 2, "Emanationism," investigates those elements which appear to constitute the backbone of the Brethren's intellectual system. It deals with issues such as the making of the world, the creation of time, the place of man in the great chain of being, and the reason why individual souls may hope to re-join their divine principle some day in the future.
- Chapter 3, "Millenarianism," looks at the way in which the Brethren used the controversial art of astrology to justify a particularly esoteric view of world history made up of prophetic cycles and completed by the coming of a messiah. More specifically, this chapter aims at clarifying how the Brethren situated their own undertaking with respect to the present cycle.

- Chapter 4, "Encyclopaedism," explores the extraordinary efforts made by the Ikhwan to impose a coherent structure on the entire body of human knowledge and, consequently, to use their epistles as a program of moral and spiritual initiation intended for their followers.
- Chapter 5, "Syncretism," examines the Brethren's impressive open-mindedness and eclecticism shown by their use of sources as they attempted to reunite the truth revealed in the sacred texts with the scientific and philosophical discoveries accumulated over the ages by scholars from throughout the world.
- Chapter 6, "Idealism," focuses on the Brethren's conception of their own cause, emphasizing their resolutely elitist approach and noting their preference for thought over action. Both points suggest that their propaganda never was intended to lead to a religious revolution, let alone a political upheaval.

At the end of the book, the Epilogue seeks to evaluate the influence that the work exerted in the following centuries.

It is clear that the avenues taken in these chapters in no way exhaust the vast and complex range of issues raised by the Brethren of Purity and their Epistles. The book will have achieved its aim, however, if it reaches beyond the usual circle of experts to introduce a new audience to the dizzy heights of a group of thinkers firmly committed to saving humankind's intellectual heritage for posterity.

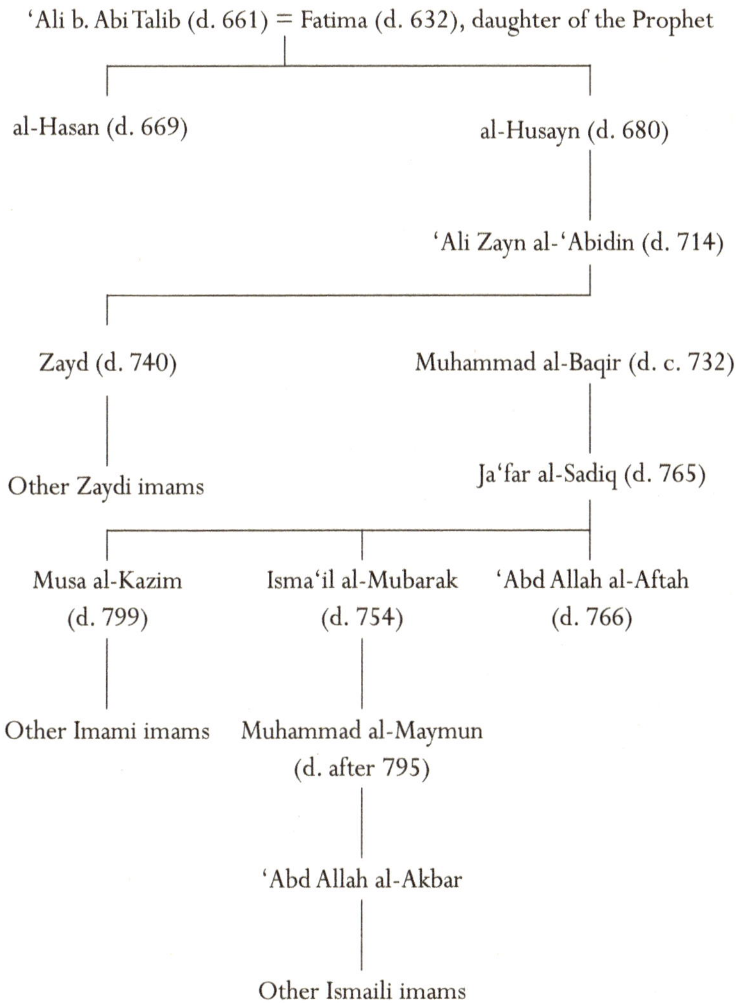

First Imami and Ismaili Imams

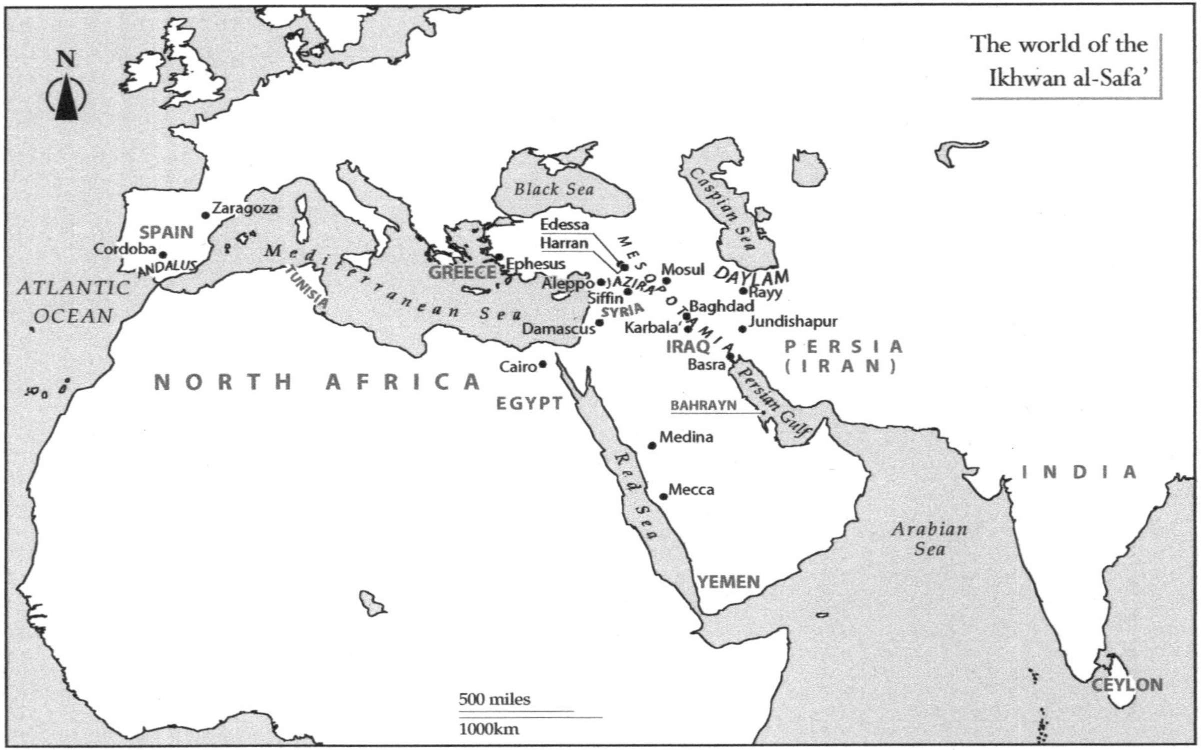

Map by MAPgrafix

1

ESOTERICISM

> Know, my pious and merciful brother (May God stand by you, as well as by ourselves, with a spirit coming from Him!), that we, the group of the Brethren of Purity and pure and noble friends, have been asleep in the Cave of our father Adam for a long time, enduring the vicissitudes of time and the misfortunes of existence (*R*. IV, 18).

Reading the Epistles of the Brethren of Purity is a curious experience. On the one hand, one rapidly notes that the authors are doing everything they can to remain anonymous – an effort in which they succeeded all too well – and, on the other hand, one soon develops a sense of familiarity, indeed intimacy, with them. To a large extent, this feeling of proximity is due to the literary genre, namely a set of scientific treatises in the form of individual epistles, and perhaps even more to the tone, which was certainly meant to be friendly, although it is understandable that some people have found it unbearably patronizing in places: "Know, my brother (May God stand by you, as well as by ourselves, with a spirit coming from Him!), that…" is beyond any doubt the most common expression in the entire corpus, as it appears at the beginning of innumerable paragraphs of this two-thousand-page work.

This is a work in which the reader is being called a brother (*akh*), indeed a younger brother, without knowing whose brother he is. His brothers, or more exactly brethren (*ikhwan*), endlessly call upon him to learn from them a message that has been prepared and written down for his sake. They treat the reader as someone who has been chosen for membership of their community and who may therefore hope to be blessed by God, but they constantly remind him of his primary duty, which is "to know." The authors called themselves the Brethren of Purity (*Ikhwan al-Safa'*), and this was clearly a well-chosen name, not only because they could hide behind it, but also because it could mean many different things at the same time. As one quickly begins to realize, the "Brethren of Purity" are simultaneously the authors of the Epistles, their readers, and all those who share, have shared, or will some day come to share their views and adhere to the program of the brotherhood.

THE NAME

The name behind which the authors hid was not just accommodating, but also loaded with symbolic significance. According to Goldziher, the expression *Ikhwan al-Safa'* comes from the story of the ring-dove and her companions in the *Kalila wa-Dimna,* originally an Indian collection of animal fables which had been translated into Pahlavi (middle Persian) before the rise of Islam, and which was later translated into Arabic by the famous secretary Ibn al-Muqaffa' (d. 759). The story tells of how a ring-dove which had been caught in a fowler's net was saved by the intervention of a rat, which gnawed the net. It is the first of several stories in which animals benefit from the help of their "pure brethren" (*ikhwan al-safa'*), meaning their loyal friends, those whom they could count upon to offer them assistance in a spirit of mutual help. The fables appealed greatly to our authors. They dedicate an entire treatise, Epistle 45, to the "Relations between the Brethren of Purity, their mutual help, and the sincerity of their sympathy and affection for what is religion and what makes this world." They also stress the importance of mutual friendship in another epistle (Epistle 2), in which they insist that it is impossible to achieve spiritual salvation on one's own, and here they actually urge their readers "to ponder the story of the ring-dove told in the Book *Kalila wa-Dimna*, and how it escaped from the net because it knew the truth of what we say" (*R.* I, 100).

Modern translators debate whether one should translate the word *safa'* as "sincerity" rather than "purity" (its literal meaning), but it does not really matter. Either way, it is clear that what they have in mind is true friendship, unflinching loyalty, and mutual help as practiced by the animals in the fable. They frequently refer to themselves not just as *Ikhwan al-safa'*, but also as *Khillan al-wafa* ("the Loyal Friends"), and characterize themselves by other epithets highlighting nobility and justice. Nor is there much point in debating whether one should refer to the work as the "Book" (*Kitab*), as do some of the oldest manuscripts, or as the "Epistles" (*Rasa'il*), the more common title today. For the sake of convenience, I shall refer throughout to the work as the Epistles and to the authors as the Brethren of Purity.

THE PROBLEM OF DATE AND AUTHORSHIP

It is a good deal more important to determine who the authors were, and when, where, and how they wrote. Unfortunately, it is also a good deal more difficult, as the internal evidence is extremely limited. All the epistles are presented as the work of the same brotherhood, except for Epistle 48 ("The modalities of the call to go to God"), formulated as if from an imam to his followers. The style is the same throughout, including in the letter supposedly written by the imam. The Brethren usually speak in the first person plural, but occasionally we find the first person singular, as for example in Epistle 31 ("The difference in languages, graphic figures and expressions"). Are we then to infer that this epistle was composed by a single author, whose attempt to sound like a group had failed? If so, is there a single author behind every chapter, or even behind the entire work, or was it at least supervised by a single authority? The internal evidence will not tell us.

What it will tell us is simply that the work was composed in Iraq between, at a rough estimate, the end of the ninth and the beginning of the eleventh centuries. That much is certain. Slightly less certain, but still fairly uncontroversial, are a number of further inferences made by scholars such as Diwald, Marquet, and Pinès on the basis of the following facts. The authors mention the theological school named after Ash'ari, who died in 936. They also have a passage on the twelve qualifications of the ideal ruler which strongly resembles those in the *The Virtuous City* by Farabi (d. 950). They also cite far too many verses by the great poet al-Mutanabbi (d. 965) to make it plausible that these verses were interpolated later into the texts. As these scholars observe, these features indicate that the Brethren wrote no earlier than the second half of the tenth century.

ANCIENT EVIDENCE

Fortunately, however, we also have some external evidence, of a rather high quality, from three sources which are virtually contemporary with the Epistles, and at the same time reasonably trustworthy.

The first and most important is the "Book of Pleasure and Conviviality" (*Kitab al-imta' wa'l-mu'anasa*) by the *litterateur* Abu Hayyan al-Tawhidi (d. 1023). To some extent, this source owes its value to the incidental character of the passage mentioning the Ikhwan al-Safa'. Tawhidi tells of how the vizier Ibn Sa'dan, who held office from 983 to 985 (or 986) and for whom he was working at the time, asked him what he thought about a government secretary by the name of Zayd b. Rifa'a. The vizier himself did not like this man, finding him somewhat vainglorious, but Tawhidi replies by praising his superior intelligence and knowledge – as well he might, since Zayd b. Rifa'a was among those who had recommended him to the vizier for employment. Even so, Tawhidi sounds a different note when the vizier asks which school of thought (*madhhab*) Zayd belongs to and which kind of intellectual affiliation he has. The relevant passage begins with the following words:

> One cannot assign him to any such thing as a group, because of his excited nature and ebullience in every domain, and one cannot tell what comes from the breadth of his insight and what from his

> powerful tongue. He lived in Basra for a long time and met there a group of people devoted to all kinds of sciences and arts, among them Abu Sulayman Muhammad b. Mashar al-Busti, known as al-Maqdisi, Abu'l-Hasan 'Ali b. Harun al-Zanjani, Abu Ahmad al-Nahrajuri, al-'Awfi, and others. He kept their company and served them. The group was characterized by harmonious relations and pure friendship and met on the basis of holiness, purity, and sincere advice. Between them, they established a doctrine by which, they claimed, they would be able to get closer to winning God's approval and traveling to His Paradise. For they used to say: "The Revelation [literally "the Law"] has been soiled by ignorance and mixed with error. There is no way to wash and purify it except through philosophy, which unites the wisdom of the creed with the benefit of rational endeavour."
>
> Perfection would be reached, they held, when Greek philosophy and Arab Revelation were joined. They composed fifty epistles on all parts of philosophy, both theoretical and practical, and attached a "Table of Contents" (*Fihrist*) to them, calling them the "Epistles of the Brethren of Purity and Loyal Friends" (*Imta'*, ii, 4–5).

This looks like a standard presentation of the Brethren and their work. A more personal appreciation on Tawhidi's part is found in the subsequent lines:

> Keeping their names secret, they circulated their epistles among the book-dealers, and instructed people in them. All this, they claimed, they did for the sake of God's face and His approval, to deliver people from corrupt doctrines which harm their souls, bad creeds which harm those who subscribe to them, and blameworthy actions which render miserable those who engage in them. They have stuffed these epistles with religious words, parables from the Revelation, made up expressions, and methods conducive to illusion. (*Imta'*, ii, 5)

In other words, the Epistles were composed by a group of idealists who saw themselves as called upon to purify Islam, based on Revelation and expressed above all in a law, by combining it with philosophy of Greek derivation. Al-Tawhidi does not approve of their enterprise, and he is even more critical in what follows. Asked whether he has seen the *Rasa'il* personally, he says that he has seen some of them, enough to conclude that the work is a jumble in which bits of truth are overwhelmed by a mass of error. He mentions that he showed a number of these epistles to Abu Sulayman al-Mantiqi (d. c. 985), his own master and friend and a well-known philosopher, and that Abu Sulayman's verdict was also negative: the authors had expended a great deal of labor on what was ultimately a futile enterprise, for the truths of philosophy and those based on revelation simply did not have anything to do with each other. Others before them had tried to combine them, he said, possibly with reference to Iranian Ismailis such as Abu Hatim al-Razi (d. 934) and Nasafi (d. 943), but they too had failed, though they were much better equipped for the task than the group from Basra. That the Basrans and also, if correctly identified, their predecessors were Shi'ites is not mentioned.

The second source is the tenth-century Mu'tazilite 'Abd al-Jabbar (d. 1025), who worked as a judge in Rayy at the end of the tenth century and whose testimony was first noted by Stern. In his "Confirmation of the Proofs of Prophethood" (*Tathbit dala'il al-nubuwwa*), a polemical work directed above all against Ismailis, 'Abd al-Jabbar rails against people who supposedly "hide" behind (Ismaili) Shi'ism and whose real views, he thinks, are that the Prophet was a trickster whose religion is about to come to an end. Among such people he mentions the judge al-Zanjani, "who is one of their chiefs and among whose followers there are secretaries and highly-placed men." He gives the names of some of these followers a bit further on: "We have singled out this Qadi al-Zanjani," he observes, "since he is a great man amongst them. Among his followers belong Zayd b. Rifa'a the secretary, Abu Ahmad al-Nahrajuri, al-'Awfi, and Abu Muhammad b. Abi'l-Baghl, secretary and astronomer. All these are residents of Basra and are still alive: others there are, in places other than Basra."

Four of these men also figure in al-Tawhidi's list, though one of al-Tawhidi's names, Abu Sulayman al-Busti (known as al-Maqdisi), is missing, and another, Muhammad b. Abi'l-Baghl, secretary and astronomer, is new. There can be no doubt that the reference here is to the same group as that described by al-Tawhidi, and here we are left in no doubt about their Shi'ism. But this time their Epistles are not mentioned.

The third source is Abu Sulayman al-Mantiqi (also known as al-Sijistani), the philosopher and teacher of al-Tawhidi whom al-Tawhidi quoted above. We also have a statement from him on the Epistles, preserved in an epitome of his history of Greek and Islamic philosophers known as "The Cabinet of Wisdom" (*Siwan al-hikma*). He does not say anything about the brotherhood or their Shi'ism here. What he does say is that all "fifty-one epistles" were written by a single man, Abu Sulayman al-Maqdisi (al-Busti).

All in all, this is impressive evidence. It could of course have been better. Most obviously, 'Abd al-Jabbar singles out the judge Zanjani as the leader of the group and does not even mention Abu Sulayman al-Maqdisi/al-Busti, who figures as the sole author of the Epistles in our third source. But then 'Abd al-Jabbar does not mention the Epistles either. His concern is with a group of people, not with a literary work, and al-Zanjani could well have been the founder or thinking head of the brotherhood without being the sole or main author. He is characterized as "the leader of the doctrine" (*sahib al-madhhab*) in another passage of the *Imta'* in which al-Tawhidi tells a story that appears also in the Epistles, and says that he has it from him. More information about the careers of the people named, not to mention their functions in the brotherhood, would have helped us identify them.

But our three sources do give us a good idea of the kind of people we are dealing with. The founders and principal members of the brotherhood are persons of standing, two of them civil servants, one of them a judge, and all seem to be men of letters with a predilection for philosophy and science. They live in the city of Basra, where they have their meetings. They are Shi'ite, and their aim is to promote a synthesis of revealed religion and philosophy, convinced that the Revelation is in need of cleansing by rationalist means, which 'Abd al-Jabbar took to mean that they were enemies of Islam. In pursuit of their aim they have compiled fifty or fifty-one epistles on all parts of what they call philosophy, published them, and tried to gain adherents for their ideas. All this fits perfectly with what we can tell from the Epistles themselves. It does not however help us decide how the Brethren divided the labor between them. Was al-Maqdisi/Busti the man who occasionally forgot to masquerade as a group in Epistle 31? If so, did he really write the entire work or did Epistle 31 just form part of his assignment? We know no better than before.

LATER CONJECTURES

Later sources do not tell us any more about the authors than our first three. What they add are distortions, which get worse and worse as the centuries roll by. But they are interesting for showing that the Ismailis began to claim them as their own.

When 'Abd al-Jabbar identified the brotherhood as Ismaili, he did not distinguish between the very different branches into which Ismailism had come to be divided by his time. To him, it was all the same abominable heresy whatever its subdivisions. The difference matters for us, however, for although 'Abd al-Jabbar may well be right that the authors were Ismailis of some kind or other, they did not apparently subscribe to Ismailism of the Fatimid variety, represented by the Fatimid caliphs of North Africa and Egypt (909–1171). The Epistles seem to have remained unknown to the Fatimid Ismailis. The Fatimids eventually disappeared, leaving behind a number of offshoots, and it was among these offshoots that the *Rasa'il* came to be known and so well loved that the authors were counted among their patriarchs.

One source to claim them as such, arguably the oldest one at our disposal, belongs to the Syrian community of the Nizaris – those Ismailis who are known in Western literature since the time of the Crusades as the Assassins. The work is ascribed to a Nizari propagandist or missionary (*da'i*) who was murdered in Aleppo shortly after 1100, and the passage of interest was identified and translated by Stern. It speaks of those who "collaborated in composing long epistles, fifty-two in number, on various branches of learning," and identifies them with the earliest missionaries of the movement, who died when Muhammad, the son of Isma'il (d. before 765), died and "his authority passed to his son, 'Abd Allah b. Muhammad, the hidden one, who was the first to hide himself from his contemporary adversaries, since his epoch was one of interruption and trial, and the Abbasid usurpers searched for those (of the imams) whose identity was known, out of envy and hatred towards the Friends of God."

We begin to find references to the Epistles from the middle of the twelfth century, frequently along with long and respectful quotations, in the writings of another branch of Ismailism, the Tayyibis in Yemen. And from the late twelfth or early thirteenth centuries onwards, Tayyibi authors tell us that the Epistles were composed by an imam, more precisely the second imam in hiding, Ahmad b. 'Abd Allah b. Muhammad b. Isma'il, who had gone into hiding to escape persecution by the Abbasid caliph Ma'mun (r. 813–833). Tayyibi authors even came to identify the Epistles as "the Qur'an of the Imams" (Stern, 1983: 170).

According to the Sunni historian Ibn al-Qifti (d. 1248), there were also people who ascribed the Epistles to the Imam Ja'far al-Sadiq (d. 765), venerated by both Imami and Ismaili Shi'ites, or even to 'Ali (d. 661), venerated by Shi'ites of all types and Sunnis alike. We do not know where these ascriptions originated. The same is true of the claim, also mentioned by Ibn al-Qifti, that the Epistles were composed by some early Mu'tazilite theologian, though it is tempting to trace this to a Sunni traditionalist to whom everything that smacked of rationalism was the same. The ascription can hardly have been meant as a compliment. In a less absurd vein, there were also some who ascribed the authorship of the Epistles, and above all "The Comprehensive Epistle" (*Risalat al-Jami'a*, more on this below), to the late tenth-century Spanish mathematician Maslama al-Majriti. This came about because Majriti had also been credited, again falsely, with "The Aim of the Sage" (*Ghayat al-Hakim*), an important treatise on magic which was to enjoy considerable success in the West. Pseudo-Majriti, as the author of the work on magic is known, alludes to a set of epistles he had composed, and this was understood as a reference to the Epistles of the Brethren of Purity. It was a natural assumption in view of the character of the works in question, and what is more, it was one of the genuine Maslama al-Majriti's disciples, the physician and geometer Kirmani, who had introduced the *Rasa'il Ikhwan al-Safa'* into Spain at the end of the tenth or the beginning of the eleventh century.

But the confusion was not to stop there. The fourteenth-century Sunni scholar Safadi lists the candidates for the authorship of the Epistles as 'Ali, Ja'far al-Sadiq, the great alchemist Jabir b. Hayyan (eighth century), the mystic martyr Hallaj (d. 922), our familiar Abu Sulayman al-Maqdisi (presumably on the basis of the *Siwan al-hikma*), and, to cap it all, the renowned Sunni theologian al-Ghazali!

MODERN CONFUSION

Not surprisingly, opinions are also divided in modern scholarship, if not perhaps to quite the same degree. Should we see the Epistles as a collective creation or the work of a single author? Most modern scholars have opted for the former answer, although some, Diwald and Netton among them, have insisted that the latter answer could be upheld with equal right. If the work was collective, should we envisage it as composed over a few years or rather as the product of a longer period of elaboration, perhaps extending over several generations? Again, most scholars opt for the former answer, but others, notably Marquet and Hamdani, have argued for the latter, in diverse ways and sometimes with changes of opinion within the work of the same scholar. In what period do we place the Epistles, or at least their beginning? Here the extremes are represented by Hamdani, who regards the work as fully completed before the year 909, when the Fatimid caliphate was established in North Africa, and Casanova, who places the work shortly before the middle of the eleventh century, based on an astrological passage. The first opinion cannot be upheld without postulating massive interpolations, while the second requires rejection of the testimonies of Tawhidi, 'Abd al-Jabbar, and Abu Sulayman al-Mantiqi examined above. For this reason, the general consensus is that the Epistles were composed in or about the 970s. They had been published by the early 980s, for the vizier with whom al-Tawhidi discussed them died in 985 or 986, and Abu Sulayman al-Mantiqi, the philosopher to whom al-Tawhidi showed them and who also wrote about them in his *Siwan al-hikma,* died about the same time.

The biggest disagreement is over the doctrinal affinities of our authors. Here the spectrum of opinion is truly varied. As Hamdani once put it: "Having taken their stand on the date of composition of the *Rasa'il*, scholars have argued whether its authors were Sunnis or Shi'is; if Sunnis, whether they were Mu'tazili or Sufi; if Shi'is, whether they were Zaydi, Ithna-'Ashari (i.e. Imami Shi'ism), Fatimid or Qarmatian" (Hamdani, 1984: 98). Today, the major confrontation seems to be between those who, following in the footsteps of Corbin and Marquet, consider the Epistles of the Brethren of Purity to be a typical work of Ismaili propaganda, and those who, like Diwald or Nasr, prefer to concentrate on the affinities between the Epistles and other groups, whether inside or outside the Islamic world, without necessarily denying the Ismaili connection. This hotchpotch of interpretations is perhaps the clearest indication of the Brethren's success in their attempt to camouflage themselves.

THE TANGIBLE CORPUS OF EPISTLES

Fortunately for us, the Epistles are of great interest even without definite answers to all the controversial questions, which I shall try to avoid as far as possible in what follows. This said, it is time to introduce the work itself. There are 51 or 52 epistles in all. Modern editions have 52, but as will be seen, things are not so simple. Their names and brief identifications are listed below as they appear in the manuscript tradition. The figures in square brackets refer to the volume and page of the four-volume edition by al-Bustani published in Beirut which, pending the completion of the first critical edition of the text now underway, is still the most commonly used throughout the world. Users of other editions should note that they can find the corresponding passages in the Cairo and Bombay editions via the key mentioned in the bibliography at the end of this book.

Section I: The mathematical sciences (14 epistles)

Epistle 1: On the number [vol. I, p. 48].
Epistle 2: The epistle entitled *jumatriya*, dealing with geometry (*handasa*), and account of its quiddity [vol. I, p. 78].
Epistle 3: The epistle entitled *asturunumiya*, dealing with the science of the stars and the composition of the spheres [vol. I, p. 114].
Epistle 4: On geography (*al-jughrafiya*) [vol. I, p. 158].
Epistle 5: On music (*al-musiqa*) [vol. I, p. 183].
Epistle 6: On the arithmetical and geometrical proportions with respect to the refinement of the soul and the reforming of characters [vol. I, p. 242].
Epistle 7: On the scientific arts and their object [vol. I, p. 258].
Epistle 8: On the practical arts and their object [vol. I, p. 276].
Epistle 9: On the explanation of characters, the causes of their difference, their types of diseases, and anecdotes drawn from the refined manners of the Prophets and the cream of the morals of the sages [vol I, p. 296].
Epistle 10: On the *Isagoge* (*isaghuji*) [vol. I, p. 390].
Epistle 11: On the ten categories, that is, *qatighuriyas* [vol. I, p. 404].
Epistle 12: On the meaning of the *Peri Hermeneias* (*baramaniyas*) [vol. I, p. 414].
Epistle 13: On the meaning of the Analytics (*anulutiqa*) [vol. I, p. 420].
Epistle 14: On the meaning of the Posterior Analytics (*anulutiqa al-thaniya*) [vol. I, p. 429].

Section II: The corporeal and natural sciences (17 epistles)

Epistle 15: Where one accounts for the matter, the form, the motion, the time and the place, together with the meanings of these [things] when they are linked to each another [vol. II, p. 5].
Epistle 16: The epistle entitled "The heavens and the world," on the reforming of the soul and the refinement of the characters [vol. II, p. 24].

Epistle 17: Where one accounts for the coming-to-be and the passing-away [vol. II, p. 52].
Epistle 18: On meteors [vol. II, p. 62].
Epistle 19: Where one accounts for the coming-to-be of the minerals [vol. II, p. 87].
Epistle 20: On the quiddity of nature [vol. II, p. 132].
Epistle 21: On the kinds of plants [vol. II, p. 150].
Epistle 22: On the modalities of the coming-to-be of the animals and of their kinds [vol. II, 178].
Epistle 23: On the composition of the corporeal system [vol. II, p. 378].
Epistle 24: On the sense and the sensible, with respect to the refinement of the soul and the reforming of the characters [vol. II, p. 396].
Epistle 25: On the place where the drop of sperm falls [vol. II, p. 417].
Epistle 26: On the claim of the sages that man is a microcosm [vol. II, p. 456].
Epistle 27: On the modalities of birth of the particular souls in the natural corporeal systems of man [vol. III, p. 5].
Epistle 28: Where one accounts for the capacity of man to know, which limit he [can] arrive at, what he [can] grasp of the sciences, which end he arrives at and which nobility he raises to [vol. III, p. 18].
Epistle 29: On the point of death and birth [vol. III, p. 34].
Epistle 30: On what is particular to pleasures; on the wisdom of birth and death and the quiddity of them both [vol. III, P; 52].
Epistle 31: On the reasons of the difference in languages, graphic figures and expressions [vol. III, p. 84].

Section III: The sciences of the soul and of the intellect (10 epistles)

Epistle 32: On the intellectual principles of the existing beings according to the Pythagoreans [vol. III, p. 178].

Epistle 33: On the intellectual principles according to the Brethren of Purity [vol. III, p. 199].
Epistle 34: On the meaning of the claim of the sages that the world is a *macranthrope* [vol. III, p. 212].
Epistle 35: On the intellect and the intelligible [vol. III, p. 231].
Epistle 36: On revolutions and cycles [vol. III, p. 249].
Epistle 37: On the quiddity of love [vol. III, p. 269].
Epistle 38: On rebirth and resurrection [vol. III, p. 287].
Epistle 39: On the quantity of the kinds of motions [vol. III, p. 321].
Epistle 40: On causes and effects [vol. III, p. 344].
Epistle 41: On definitions and descriptions [vol. III, p. 384].

Section IV: The nomic, divine, and legal sciences (11 epistles)

Epistle 42: On views and religions [vol. III, p. 401].
Epistle 43: On the quiddity of the Way [leading] to God – How Powerful and Lofty is He! [vol. IV, p. 5].
Epistle 44: Where one accounts for the belief of the Brethren of Purity and the doctrine of the divine men [vol. IV, p. 14].
Epistle 45: On the modalities of the relations of the Brethren of Purity, their mutual help and the authenticity of the sympathy and affection [they have for each other], whether it be for the religion or for what is pertaining to this world [vol. IV, p. 41].
Epistle 46: On the quiddity of faith and the characteristics of the believers who realise [those things] [vol. IV, p. 61].
Epistle 47: On the quiddity of the divine "nomos," the conditions of prophecy and the quantity of the characteristics [of the Prophets]; on the doctrines of the divine men and of the men of God [vol. IV, p. 124].
Epistle 48: On the modalities of the call [to go] to God [vol. IV, p. 145].
Epistle 49: On the modalities of the states of the spiritual beings [vol. IV, p. 198].

Epistle 50: On the modalities of the species of governance and of their quantity [vol. IV, p. 250].
Epistle 51: On the modalities of the arrangement of the world as a whole [vol. IV, p. 273].
Epistle 52: On the quiddity of magic, incantations and the evil eye [vol. IV, p. 283].

There are good reasons for suspecting that one of these epistles is a later addition. In various parts of the text, it is asserted that the *Rasa'il* are fifty-one in number. What is more, the last epistle, though numbered 52, actually names itself the fifty-first and the last, and refers to the "fifty previous epistles" of the corpus. The extra epistle, as Marquet has shown, is most probably the very brief epistle that precedes it – Epistle 51 in our edition – which, in addition to being manifestly out of place, proves to be largely a word-for-word doublet of a part of Epistle 21. That brings the number of epistles down to fifty-one, which is still one more than the total mentioned by Tawhidi (though it tallies with that given by Abu Sulayman al-Mantiqi). The "Table of Contents" (*Fihrist*) added by the authors, according to Tawhidi, was not an epistle, merely a kind of index which has been preserved and can be found at the beginning of the first volume of al-Bustani's edition. But maybe Tawhidi simply meant "fifty" as a round number. There is also a problem in that we must probably add to the list of genuine epistles the so-called "Comprehensive Epistle" (*Risalat al-Jami'a*), to which there are references here and there in the corpus and which was meant, as is clear from these references, to serve as a kind of recapitulation and clarification of the rest. It does seem to have been intended as a separate work, and it is as such that it has been printed in Beirut. At all event, this "Comprehensive Epistle" is not quite what was intended, for it leaves unanswered a great number of the questions raised in the other parts of the corpus.

While it is true that we must exclude both the *Risalat al-Jami'a* and the *Fihrist* from the standard count of epistles, we are hardly to attach special importance to the number 51. According to Corbin and Marquet, it is deeply meaningful. They also found significance in the fact that the second section consists of seventeen epistles. But though it is true that the Brethren are extremely fond of numerical symbolism, this is, in my opinion, to go too far.

The overall plan of the work, the sequence of the subject-matter, and the principles behind the classification are all issues which will be dealt with in more detail later. At this stage, however, it may be noted that we have a well-balanced corpus in the sense that the four sections are of roughly equal length – they consist of fourteen, seventeen, ten, and eleven (or ten) epistles respectively – and that the epistles themselves tend to be of roughly even length as well, usually between twenty and thirty pages. But there are two remarkable exceptions. One is the very last epistle, the fifty-second, which is actually the fifty-first, and which deals with "the quiddity of magic, incantations and the evil eye." It is close to two hundred pages long in the Beirut edition. It has also provoked very different responses in modern scholars, being dismissed by some as of no great value and revered by others as the pinnacle of the entire edifice, but there are no doubts about its authenticity. The other exception is Epistle 22 ("On animals"), which is by far the longest of all once the *Risala al-Jami'a* has been left out of the computation. Most of it is taken up by a long tale, entitled "The Case of the Animals versus Man before the King of the Jinn" in a modern English translation. This is without doubt the most famous part of the whole corpus. It was translated into languages as diverse as Hebrew, Persian, Turkish, and Hindustani in pre-modern times and has now been translated into English and German. There are good reasons for its popularity, since it is a very diverting piece of literature on its own, in addition to having a clearly metaphorical resonance. But exceptional though Epistle 22 is in terms of length, it is part and parcel of the Epistles, and it would certainly be a mistake for anyone trying to understand the Brethren's work as a whole to consider it apart from the rest of the collection.

2

EMANATIONISM

> Now consider, my brother (May God stand by you, as well as by ourselves, with a spirit coming from Him!) the way your soul will pass on from this world to that place. For your soul is one of those faculties that are spread from the World Soul circulating in the world. It has already reached the center, departed from it and escaped from being in minerals, plants and animals. It has overstepped the reverted path and the curved path alike, and is now on the upright path, which is the last degree of Hell, for this is the human shape (*R.* II, 183).

Whoever sets out to read the *Rasa'il* must be prepared endlessly to move back and forth between, as it were, the two "poles" of a same structure, one the human being, the other the divine principle to which it hopes to return. Where does man come from? Which place does he occupy in the creation? Is it so that he may contemplate the idea of becoming one again with a divine principle? These are the questions that preoccupy the Brethren from the beginning to the end of the corpus. Their answers will be discussed here.

THE FORMATION OF THE UNIVERSE

At the core of the Brethren's synthesis lies the theory of emanation. Like the Neoplatonists, the Ikhwan conceived of the world we know as the result of a process whereby all beings flowed or "emanated" (*fada*), like a light, from the original principle, namely the Primeval

Unity or, more simply still, the One. Plotinus (d. 270), the founder of Neoplatonism, postulated a series of three successive principles, named hypostases, before and above matter. The first was the One, the source of all beings, that is, what a Christian, a Jew, or a Muslim would call God or the transcendent Creator, but not actually conceived as a personal being. The second was the Intellect, another concept that should not be envisaged as a person. Rather, it was a principle embodying divine reason or intelligence. It was also the archetype of the world, perfect by nature yet necessarily distinct from the One. The last was the Soul, which embodied life. Its primary function was to move the material world (once it had come into existence) and to bring it into conformity with its spiritual archetype in so far as possible.

The Brethren took up the Plotinian scheme more or less without change, but like other Neoplatonists such as Iamblichus (d. 326), they extended and developed it so as to integrate a greater number of levels of realities or, as they would rather put it, "limits" (*hudud*) in the hierarchy of beings. As we shall see, they modeled their own theory of emanation (*fayd*) on the nine fundamental units of that other great chain known as the theory of numbers. In doing so, they clearly aligned themselves with Pythagoras (sixth century BCE) and his followers, who held that numbers were important for their qualitative properties and symbolic significance at least as much as for their quantitative values.

Although it pervades most of their corpus, the Brethren's emanation scheme is actually discussed in only two epistles. These are Epistle 32, purposefully entitled "The intellectual principles of existing beings according to the Pythagoreans," and Epistle 49, named "The modalities of the states of the spiritual beings." Here the Brethren begin by presenting their own version of the triad of spiritual principles they found in Plotinus. In the first place is the One, the divine source of everything, which is perfect, eternal, transcendent, and, of course, unique by definition. Our authors explicitly identify this principle with the Creator (*al-Bari*) of all beings, referred to as God in the sacred scriptures. This should not come as a surprise, given that Christian Neoplatonists had already done this, but though the One thus became a being, he was still very different from God as we know him from the scriptures. Indeed, there is something awkward even about calling this being "He," for the One as the Brethren see him is utterly unknowable. Next we find the Universal Intellect (*al-'aql*), which the Brethren define, among other things, as the all-knowing archetype of all forms of intelligible beings. This second principle is closely related to the first, sharing with it a certain number of qualities such as existence (*wujud*), eternity (*baqa'*), completeness (*tamam*), and perfection (*kamal*). And yet the Universal Intellect must be considered to be distinct from its cause, as we said, for the obvious reason that otherwise the Creator's absolute transcendence with respect to His creation could not be preserved. As experts in metaphorical language, the Brethren illustrate this point by stating that the Intellect is at the same time the great veil hiding God and the great door leading to His Oneness. In the third place comes the World Soul (*al-nafs*), by which the material world was planned to be generated, moved, and organized according to the virtues which the Soul will keep receiving from the Intellect. This World Soul, the Ikhwan tell us, is living and active by nature, but it is knowing and perfect only in power, that is to say, only to the extent that it succeeds in maintaining and transmitting the flow it gets from the Intellect. To account for the World Soul's decisive role in the genesis of the universe, Plato described its twofold composition, stating in a famous passage of his *Timaeus* that it was made of an indivisible principle ("the Same") and a divisible principle ("the Other") at the same time. In different words but from essentially the same perspective, the Brethren speak of the World Soul's split between its superior and inferior parts, which they call "the Head" and "the Tail" respectively. Thanks to the former, they write, the Soul is able to contemplate the nobility and absolute perfection of the realities above itself, but the latter makes it turn towards the lower beings of the material world instead. Whatever image is used, it is obvious that the World Soul plays a crucial role in the emanation scheme, as it marks the all-important transition from the spiritual to the material and sensible world. As for matter, which is still deprived of its dimensions and directions, the Brethren call it the Prime Matter (*al-hayula 'l-ula*) and give it the fourth rank in the sequence, as we would expect.

The rest of the scheme is decisively more original. In a language abundant in vivid expressions but, it would seem, not entirely free of contradictions, the Brethren narrate how the Soul's tail eventually came to form a faculty of its own, namely Nature (*al-tabi'a*), which was to take the fifth rank in the sequence and act as the cause of change in the world here below. Next, how the Soul as a whole mated with Prime Matter so as to produce the Absolute Body (*al-jism al-mutlaq*) or "Second Matter," that is, the corporeal world, by now endowed with three dimensions. It is at this stage (rank 6), our authors add, that the material world received its spherical shape from the Soul. The next stage in the process (rank 7) was when the Sphere (*al-falak*) was divided to constitute the heavenly spheres, which the World Soul then set in motion.

THE CREATION OF TIME

This was no doubt also an event of great significance in the emanation process, for it meant nothing less than the invention of time. Once again in fairly good agreement with the cosmological background of Plato's *Timaeus*, the Brethren appear to accept the definition of time as "a moving image of eternity." What is beyond doubt is that they adopt his view that the planets are "the instruments of time" and, more obviously still, that they set a high value on the concept commonly referred to as the "Great Platonic Year." Plato defined the Great Year, or rather the Perfect Year, as the period required for all the heavenly spheres, namely the seven planetary spheres (that is, Saturn, Jupiter, Mars, the Sun, Venus, Mercury, and the Moon) and the starry sphere to come back into conjunction. Planets are said to be in conjunction when they occupy identical positions in their respective spheres, one behind the other, like the Sun and the Moon at times of eclipses. Each planet moves around in its sphere like a hand around the dial of the clock, and the occurrence of conjunctions depends on the time it takes for the planets involved to complete their respective revolutions. There are many of these conjunctions (the Ikhwan cite the figure of 43,200!), each one determining a specific cycle, but the greatest of all celestial cycles will only be completed when all the spheres come back to exactly the same positions that they held in the beginning. Implicit in Plato's theory was the idea that the planets had been in a general conjunction with the starry sphere in the beginning of the universe. He did not explicitly assign a length to the conjunctional Great Year. The Brethren, however, are perfectly explicit on both points. Undoubtedly influenced by cosmological speculations from India, they state that the first impetus occurred when all planets were in general conjunction at the first degree of Aries and in various points in the Epistles they assign the cycle a period of 360,000 years. As we shall later have more opportunities to go into the detail of the Brethren's own speculations about time, we can now return to the emanation scheme and see what the further ranks of beings are made of.

COMING-TO-BE AND PASSING-AWAY

The Ikhwan also adopt the traditional belief that the world of coming-to-be and passing-away (*'alam al-kawn wa-l-fasad*), i.e. the world in which we live, fills the sphere below the Moon (the sublunar sphere). In agreement with one of the most standard tenets of ancient Greek physics, they thus assume that the world was originally made of only the four basic elements (*al-arkan*) of nature – namely, Fire, Air, Water, and ultimately Earth at the center of the universe – but the mixing of their humors (hot-dry, hot-wet, cold-wet, and cold-dry respectively) with one another later resulted in the three phases by which minerals, plants, and animals were successively brought into being. Accordingly, the Brethren assign the eighth position to the four elements at the time when their humors were still separated from each other, and the ninth and ultimate one to the three kingdoms of "generated Beings" (*al-muwalladat*) that came to be produced in succession at a later stage. As a necessary implication of the emanation theory, every being under the sphere of the Moon is said to possess an individual soul, yet these sub-lunar souls differ from one another in terms of the species of beings to which they belong. Thus, while the mineral soul's only faculty is its ability to come-to-be and pass-away, the vegetal soul has the additional power of nutrition and growth, and the animal soul has the further abilities to feel and to move in space. So although minerals came before plants, and plants before animals, the order is the opposite in terms of nobility. It is telling that the ontological hierarchy of beings no longer coincides with the chronological sequence, for it looks like an indispensable prerequisite of man's appearance on the scene. The first part of the Brethren's scheme operates on the assumption that nobility and chronological priority go together: the highest beings were the first. Now the relationship is reversed: the first beings are the most primitive, minerals are less developed than plants, which are less developed than animals. This reversal is clearly required to make man the noblest being in the sub-lunar world.

THE PLACE OF MAN IN GOD'S CREATION

In spite of this, human beings do not receive a status of their own in the Ikhwan's hierarchy, as they occupy the same rank as minerals, plants, and animals; that is the ninth and last of the scheme. Human beings are animals. As all animals, they are able to feel and to move. Yet what makes their genus so different from all other creatures in this world is that they are the only ones to possess rational souls in addition to the vegetative and animal faculties. The Brethren account for this superiority by stating that mankind was also the last to appear in the world of coming-to-be and passing-away. Some modern writers have been tempted to see in this view some kind of pre-Darwinian theory of evolution, but this proposal makes no sense at all, as was rightly pointed out by Nasr, for it completely overlooks the teleological perspective of the Brethren's whole scheme. It was God's will to create the world, the Ikhwan write, and it is fitting that His perfection and wisdom be reflected in His creation. Imperfection exists in this world, but it arises from causes which are accidental, not essential. The general order of things cannot be other than good, as is necessarily also the Creator's intention that man be the ultimate being in the creation. As the Qur'an says, he is also the one which received "the best of all constitutions" (Q. 95:4), and it was man that God appointed as His own "caliph on earth" (Q. 2:30). In fact, man could almost be defined as the very purpose of creation, although the Brethren seem to have refrained from explicit use of this kind of expression. But they assume that plants have been created to feed animals and animals to serve mankind, thereby implying that man is the final objective to which the rest of creation naturally leads.

Now and then, the Ikhwan emphasize man's likeness to his Creator, an attitude not particularly surprising given the authors' general familiarity with biblical material. Yet, more in line with one of the most unquestionable creeds of Islam, namely God's absolute transcendence, they seem to show a much greater preference for comparing man with other elements of the creation. They could draw upon a great variety of earlier opinions, since it is a basic tenet of most ancient religions and philosophies that man is a sort of miniature of the world. The Brethren duly acknowledge their own debt in that field, most conspicuously in Epistles 26 and 34, which bear the explicit titles of "The claim of the sages that man is a microcosm (*'alam saghir*, literally 'small world')" and "The meaning of the claim of the sages that the world is a 'macranthrope' (*insan kabir*, literally 'big man')" respectively. In the beginning of the former, one finds the following passage, which is illustrative of their method:

> Since man is a combination of a corporeal body and a spiritual soul, they [the first sages] found correspondences, in the construction of his body, with all existing things in the corporeal world: the marvellous composition of its spheres, the divisions of its zodiacal signs, the movements of its stars, the composition of its basic elements and matrices, the different substances of its minerals, the variety of its plants, and the wonderful constitutions of its animals. They also found a similarity between the human soul and the way its powers circulate in the constitution of its body (on the one hand)

> and the various kinds of spiritual creatures – angels, jinn, humans, devils, and the souls of all the animals – and the disposition of their circumstances in this world (on the other). (*R.* II, 457)

A is to B what B is to C; A is to B what C is to D: this type of analogical reasoning was already much favored in antiquity by Plato and his followers. But the reader of the *Rasa'il* is likely to realize that the authors have made use of analogy (*qiyas*) to a degree rarely seen in earlier literature and, what is more, that man is directly concerned in most cases. By virtue of the universal sympathy found between beings sharing a common origin, the Brethren allow themselves to see correspondences between human beings (or the faculties they are said to possess) and nearly everything in God's creation, from zodiacal signs and planets to insects, colours, smells, or drugs. More often than not, the intention is merely to stress the common perfection of all elements, so that it does not really matter in which order the things are compared. Thus, in the epistle on "Revolutions and cycles," the Brethren formulate a sustained comparison between the changes to the earth's surface over the year and those affecting a woman during the four seasons of her life, but they could as well have done it the other way round. Elsewhere, as an obvious sign that twenty-eight is a perfect number (that is, equal to the sum of its factors, according to the Pythagorean definition), they point to the relationship which is bound to exist between the twenty-eight mansions of the Moon, the twenty-eight parts of the human body and the twenty-eight letters of the Arabic alphabet. The Ikhwan do not explain how these parallels may be accounted for, nor why such correspondences are to be found in so many places. They just find them natural, as they would also find it natural to say, in agreement with the ancient Protagorean adage, that "man is the measure of everything."

MAN'S DOUBLE NATURE

All beings in the sub-lunar world are made of a body and a soul, but man is the only being whose soul is spiritual or, as we have mentioned above, rational. This is a truism found at the basis of all theories about the human condition in late antiquity, and the Brethren develop it, as so often, by following Plato. Like him, they highlight the contrast between the human body and the human soul by identifying the former as a dark, corruptible, and mortal substance, and the latter as a luminous, incorruptible, and immortal principle. Like him, they stud their sayings with an impressive arsenal of images and metaphors, the soul's command over the body being successively compared to that of a landlord over his house, a rider over his horse, a farmer over his field, and so on. More typically still, they embrace with fervor the Platonic view that the body is the soul's prison, and that it is the soul's duty to seek to liberate itself from the chains of this sad condition. Earthly life is ephemeral. Sooner or later there will come a time when the body dies, as happens with every corruptible being under the sub-lunar sphere. But the soul is not perishable, so that, in a certain sense, its "real life" begins exactly when that of the body terminates. This is what the Brethren mean when they assert that "the death of the organism is the birth of the soul" (*R.* III, 32), immediately adding that this event is "like the emerging of the fetus during birth." In several places in the *Rasa'il*, the Brethren come back to this last analogy, and even develop it at times, no doubt because they deemed it particularly useful in understanding the gist of their own belief. The earthly life we live is not as "real" as our senses suggest. In fact, it greatly resembles embryonic life, which is only the preliminary phase of a more real and more significant life yet to come. That said, it remains a fact that the embryonic state is itself a crucial phase in the process, for it is obvious that what comes next depends largely on the greater or lesser perfection achieved at the moment of birth. The implication of all this in terms of moral behavior is evident, yet it looks as though the Brethren never tire of spelling it out. Throughout the Epistles, readers are warned against the dangers of attaching too much importance to the mundane affairs of the ephemeral sojourn on earth, and conversely reminded to prepare themselves for the journey to the blissful and everlasting world that comes next. There is, of course, no question of man going so far as to despise this terrestrial life, for this would be to disdain one of God's most beautiful creations – a blasphemous thought indeed. But we should make every effort to get rid of whatever we do not need to take with us into the afterlife. "Wake up, my friend, from the slumber of ignorance and the torpor of negligence!" is an admonition found *ad nauseam* in our Epistles, as it forms part of the conclusion of nearly every one of them (in addition to being used in many other places as well). Man's quest for happiness in the other world is clearly not a short and easy process, but rather one which requires patience, suffering, and endurance.

THE SIN OF THE FIRST ADAM

The Brethren are not particularly informative about the reason why the human condition is so miserable, although they clearly did not consider this a trifling issue. They merely allude to the "Sin of the First Adam" as the cause of man's present situation in a couple of passages. In Epistle 48 ("The modalities of the call to go to God") they write, for instance:

> Here we are prisoners and strangers in the prison of nature, sunk in the sea of matter, owing to a sin (*janaya*) committed by our father, the First Adam (*adam al-awwal*), as he was deceived by his enemy, the Evil One (*la'in*), when he said: "Shall I indicate for you the tree of eternity and a kingdom that never perishes (= Q. 20:120)?" (*R.* IV, 166)

What is remarkable in these few lines is that they mix expressions traditionally pertaining to two different kinds of sources. The "prison of nature" and the "sea of matter" into which the human soul is said to have "sunk" are clichés in philosophical language. The Ikhwan undoubtedly derived them from the Neoplatonic sources they had at their disposal. But what follows is inspired by the Qur'anic version of the story of Adam, from which the last sentence of the passage is cited verbatim.

Actually, the Qur'an often speaks of two "primeval sins" rather than one. The first was committed by Iblis, that is Satan or the Evil One in our quotation, who was the only one among the angels to refuse to prostrate to Adam when God commanded them to do so (Q. 7:11–12). This was a sin of sheer arrogance, which Iblis sought to justify with the claim that he was better than Adam, since he had been created from fire, whereas Adam had been created from clay. And then there is the sin of Adam himself, when he and Eve followed Iblis's advice and plucked a fruit from the forbidden tree in the garden of Paradise (Q. 7:20–22). This was rather a sin of vanity, but it is fundamentally the same kind of transgression, namely that of seeking to overstep the limit of one's condition. What makes the Qur'anic version so distinct from the biblical accounts is the continuations. Iblis is exiled, but God grants him a delay and allows him to make deceitful promises in the future (Q. 7:13–18). As for the father of mankind, Adam is chased from Paradise, but God accepts his repentance and assures him that those of his descent who follow His guidance will be saved (Q. 7:23–25). Since in their eyes Adam has been forgiven for his behavior, Muslims traditionally do not assign the same importance to the original sin as do Christians and Jews. In their heart of hearts, every sincere believer will naturally seek to "ordain what is good and abstain from what is wrong" (Q. 3:110), as the Holy Book of Islam itself enjoins them to do. But they will certainly not be obsessed with the idea that his behavior is meant to redress a sin, be it his own or that of anyone else.

In striking contrast to the majority of Muslims, the Brethren of Purity do seem to have attached great significance to the sin of Adam. There cannot be any doubt that they considered this event to be the cause of the human soul's fall to the lower stages of this world. But where exactly they situated the story of Adam in relation to their theory of emanation is anything but clear. As mentioned above, the Ikhwan do not dwell on the issue as thoroughly as one would have liked. Besides, they appear to have hidden their beliefs on this subject under a thick veil of esotericism. Rightly so, it seems, for what the reader is able to appreciate is a far cry from strict Islamic orthodoxy. To begin with, the Brethren do not speak of one Adam only, but of several different characters all named Adam. What they call "the First Adam" is the archetypal (and purely spiritual) principle of mankind, which means that this Adam ought to occupy a very high rank in the emanation scheme. But in various places they refer to the "first earthly (*turabi*) Adam," whom God created after having sat down on His throne. This Adam is also said to have appeared on a mountain – namely, Mount Yaqut in the island of Ceylon (which symbolically represents the axis of the earth) – where he soon received from God the faculty to speak and give names to all elements in creation. This allows us to regard the earthly Adam as the first individual man to have come into being in this world, that is, at the very end of the process by which minerals, plants, and animals were formed in succession. As if this were not enough, the Brethren also mention a multitude of other individual Adams, each one of whom is identified as the inaugurator of a cycle of world history, as we shall see later in greater detail. This implicitly numbers them as the second to the seventh Adam, though these expressions are not actually used. None of this makes it easier for us to clarify the emanation scheme described above, and it is just one of countless related matters that would have to be included in the overall structure – Satan's sin, for example.

ESCHATOLOGICAL PROSPECTS

Fortunately, the Epistles provide a good deal more information about the future prospects of the human soul than about its past tribulations. The third section of the *Rasa'il* includes, for instance, an entire epistle entitled "Rebirth and resurrection" (Epistle 38), which the authors themselves introduce as of especial relevance. Yet here too the reader will have to reckon with the peculiar language the Brethren use as soon as their doctrine deviates from that of the majority. It is a language abundant in metaphors and subtle allusions, sometimes even to the point of abstruseness. It is above all a language which takes full advantage of the various meanings that a word may have. Even so, however, it can be safely assumed from a global approach to the work that the Ikhwan distinguish between three kinds, or rather levels, of eschatological prospects (that is, relating to the last things). The first of these relates to the souls of individuals, and thus concerns the destiny of each particular human soul from the moment when its body passes away. The second level relates to the collective judgment of souls, said to take place at the end of each of the above-mentioned cycles of world history. The last level is about the great resurrection of all souls, which is expected to occur once, at the end of time, when the created world is annihilated and multiplicity returned to the Primeval Unity. Since these levels are essential components of the Ikhwanian doctrine as a whole, I shall deal with them in some detail.

Let us describe the individual prospect first. Here the Brethren make heavy use of expressions and images found in the Qur'an. The sacred text contains many evocative descriptions of the realities awaiting souls after death, especially in the sections (suras) revealed in Mecca. It speaks, for example, of the balance in which the good and the bad actions of every single soul will be weighed on the day of judgment. It also speaks of two paths going in opposite directions, which souls will have to take after judgment depending which scale of the balance will have proved the heavier. One path will lead the "companions of the right hand," the virtuous and noble souls, towards the blissful gardens of Paradise (*jannat al-na'im*), where they will remain forever in the company of angels. The other path will drive the "companions of the left hand," the evil and sinful souls, to the everlasting burning flames of Hell (*jahannam*), with the devils and the whole procession of infernal creatures around them. In a few places, the Qur'an refers to the Barrier (*barzakh*) as a sort of intermediary place where souls stand between the moment of death and judgment.

When the Brethren use these and other Qur'anic images, they subtly change them, in part because of their penchant for systematization. Thus, they profess to know that what will be weighed in the balance on the day of judgment are the four cardinal virtues (and as many corresponding vices) – namely: (1) knowing the realities of existing beings, (2) believing in valid opinions, (3) having good manners and praiseworthy traits of character, (4) acting properly and behaving well. But there is surely nothing heretical about this. Nor is the Brethren's depiction of the seven infernal stages (which mirror the seven celestial circles) reprehensible in itself, although it was perhaps a little audacious on their part to identify these stages with the four types of elemental matter (Earth, Water, Air, and Fire) and the three classes of composite beings (Minerals, Plants, and Animals) respectively. But when it comes to the interpretation of what *barzakh* might mean, their presentation is more likely to raise eyebrows. For as they see it, the Qur'anic Barrier is a metaphor for the cycle of successive reincarnations that an imperfect soul must endure to complete its purification before it is allowed to share the blissful status of those who have already arrived in Paradise. The concept of reincarnation is, of course, wholly extraneous to the Holy Book of Islam. But the Ikhwan could hardly do without it, as it seems to be a natural implication of the emanation theory. Pythagoras, Plato, and all their followers in antiquity had similarly admitted the existence of these post-mortem cycles of purification and various peoples were still doing so in the Brethren's time, most notably the Brahmans in India. There are issues on which the Brethren did not share the traditional reincarnation doctrine. They seem to have ruled out, for instance, the idea that bodies could be resurrected. More importantly, they also appear to have rejected the notion of metempsychosis (*tanasukh*) in the sense of a never-ending process by which a human soul may eventually be reincarnated in an animal or a vegetable. This is probably due to the fact that such a fall from grace of the human soul is hardly consistent with the Brethren's eschatological model as a whole, given that it places mankind at the head of the general ascent of souls towards the original principle.

This brings us quite naturally to the second of our three levels, namely the collective salvation of souls at the end of great cycles of world history. In agreement with much of Plato's doctrine, they propose that time is cyclical and that it has been created that way in order to be as similar as possible to eternity. They likewise assume, as we have seen, that cycles are determined not only by the individual periods of revolution of the planetary spheres, but also by the periods it takes for some of them to come back into conjunction, the greatest possible conjunction being that of all planetary spheres with the sphere of the fixed stars. Unlike Plato, but in perfect agreement with many astrologers of their time, the Brethren set a particularly high value on a series of conjunctions involving the two furthest planets of the Greek Ptolemaic system, namely Jupiter and Saturn. It goes without saying that nothing in the model set forth thus far is easily reconcilable with the letter of the Qur'an. But the worst is still to come! For the Brethren go as far as to combine these already weird speculations with a doctrine of seven-thousand-year long prophetic cycles, which seriously affects the relative significance of religions, including Islam, in the overall perspective of world history. The detail and full implication of the theory will be discussed in Chapter 3. Yet some of its elements must be presented here, as they enable us to understand better our second level of eschatological prospect. Thus the Brethren assume that, at the end of each seven-thousand-year cycle, all the incarnated souls of this cycle would be assembled and faced with a sort of minor collective day of judgment. Depending on their relative degree of purification, human souls are then allotted one of three possible destinies. Those deemed to be insufficiently purified will have to start a new cycle of reincarnation, so that they will remain in the *barzakh* (in the sense of cycles of transmigration) for at least another seven thousand years. Those of great sinners and inveterate unbelievers will not be incarnated again, but rather thrown directly into various levels of Hell, where they will become devils and forever act as vicious and tempting powers for other souls still to be incarnated. Finally, the souls whose purification is judged sufficient (and who are apparently assumed to be more numerous than those destined for Hell) will be sent to the various levels of Paradise and there become immortal angels ready to assist like-minded souls which are still in the process of purification. In general terms, therefore, one may assume that each seven-thousand-year cycle enables a vast collection of human souls to be saved from the world of coming-to-be and passing-away, which implies in turn that in the long run the number of human souls turned into angels becomes ever greater with time. Apparently, this promotion is only part of a broader mechanism, whereby the souls of lesser beings – animals, plants, and minerals – also get the opportunity to move up in the hierarchy by one rank at a time. After all, this would fit in perfectly with the Brethren's aspiration to make their system as coherent and comprehensive as possible.

This brings us to the third and last level of the Brethren's eschatology, namely the one concerned with the end of the universe. As usual, the text is not free from ambiguity, probably deliberately, so as not to scandalize the literalists of Islamic exegesis. Thus, the authors use the term "resurrection" (*qiyama*) to mean the individual soul's liberation from its corporeal chains. For the collective liberation of souls at the end of a prophetic cycle, they speak of the "great resurrection" (*al-qiyama al-kubra*), although there are times as when they call it simply "resurrection" as well. And both terms seem to be indiscriminately used to refer to yet another salvation of souls, namely that at the end of the world itself. For imprecise though their terminology may be, the Brethren leave no doubt that the world will end one day, when all souls without exception (thus including the damned souls in Hell) will rise up to dissolve in their spiritual point of origin, namely the World Soul. How exactly they envisage the final phase of the universe is not evident, but a general idea can nevertheless be inferred from various indications in the text. Time will reach its term. The celestial spheres will cease their revolutions. The material world will be destroyed, either through flood or conflagration, given that the final objective of creation will have now been reached. The World Soul, henceforward completely liberated from any corporeal substance, will re-ascend to its cause, the Intellect, and this latter in turn will be one again with its own cause, namely the Primeval Unity.

When are these apocalyptic events due to take place? The Brethren prudently avoid being too explicit. One might have expected the end of the world to coincide with the completion of the Great Year, that is, 360,000 years after the initial conjunction in Aries. But there is at least one indication in the text that the lifespan of the universe was assigned a much longer period than this. This is found in Epistle 36 ("Revolutions and cycles"), where the authors rely on an Indian source to assert that:

> Among conjunctions there is one which takes place once every 360,000 years, and this is the period from when all the planets come together, in their mean motions, in the first minute of the sign of Aries, until they come back to it once again. This revolution is called, in the *Zij al-Sindhind* "one day of the days of the Macrocosm" (*yawm wahid min ayyam al-'alam al-kabir*). (*R.* III, 251)

Should we infer from these lines that the lifespan of the universe consists of 360 × 360,000 = 129,600,000 years? Or else perhaps of 360,000 × 360,000 = 129,600,000,000 years? The Ikhwan will not tell us, nor will they disclose where the present seven-thousand-year cycle fits into these vertiginous measurements.

3

MILLENARIANISM

> Among the features of our Brethren is that they are learned in the field of religion, that they know the secrets of prophecies and that they are well-trained in the philosophical disciplines. When you meet one of them and seem to note integrity in him, tell him something that will please him and remind him of the recommencement of the revolution of revealing and awakening, as well as of the dissipation of worries for mankind, from the transfer of the conjunction, from the sign of fiery triplicities to the sign of vegetal and animal triplicities, in the tenth circle which corresponds to the house of power and the appearance of the eminent people (*R.* IV, 146).

Let us consider once again the list of the Epistles that we discussed at the end of Chapter 1. Whereas one science is ordinarily dealt with in one epistle, we see that the science of the heavens is dealt with in at least three. Astronomy, one of the disciplines of the Pythagorean *quadrivium* alongside arithmetic, geometry, and music, finds its proper place in the third epistle of the first section, on mathematics. An epistle on "The heavens and the world" (Epistle 16) also appears in the second section, on the natural sciences, as one would expect. Finally, the Brethren dedicate an entire epistle to "Revolutions and cycles" (Epistle 36) in the third section, on the sciences of the soul and the intellect. On top of that, many other epistles contain large portions of text directly concerned with astronomical or, more commonly, astrological issues. Paramount in this last respect is the long epistle on magic which concludes the fourth section, on the divine and legal sciences, and with which the entire corpus comes to an end. So it is clearly not an exaggeration to claim that the science of the heavens pervades the entire corpus of the *Rasa'il*.

ASTROLOGICAL DETERMINISM

In order to understand what the Brethren mean by the science of the heavens we need to look briefly at the main ideas in the epistles in which they discuss it, that is, Epistles 3, 16, and 36.

Epistle 3 ("Astronomy") begins with the definition of the three parts which make up the "sciences of the stars" (*'ilm al-nujum*). In the first place comes study of the composition of heavenly spheres, the number of stars, the divisions of zodiacal signs, together with the study of the distances, the sizes, and the movements of all those bodies. This first part, which the Brethren call the "science of the exterior shape (of the heavens)" (*'ilm al-hay'a*), should thus be identified with what we now call cosmology. In the second place comes a science to which the Brethren do not give a name. They define it as the science of tables, calendars, and the calculating of eras. The last part is "the knowledge of the ways to draw indications for things that come-to-be, before their coming-to-be under the sphere of the Moon, from the ascendants of the zodiacal signs and the movements of the stars, thanks to the revolution of the sphere." This the Brethren term "the science of the (celestial) decrees" (*'ilm al-ahkam*), which was one of the most common Arabic expressions for what we would now call astrology.

The first few pages of the treatise do not claim to do more than sum up a number of astronomical "verities" which had been widely accepted since the time of the Greeks and transmitted almost without change since Ptolemy's *Almagest*, composed in the second century CE. These verities include observations such as that there are in all 1029 stars, all seemingly fixed to the celestial sphere save seven, which appear to wander on a sphere of their own and which for that reason are called planets (Greek *planetes*, from *planasthai*, to wander). In the geocentric model inherited from the ancients, in which the Earth is the centre of the universe, the order of the planets is Moon, Mercury, Venus, Sun, Mars, Jupiter, and Saturn. Now to account for the movement of equinoctial precession – whose discovery is usually ascribed to Hipparchus in the second century BCE – it was customary to postulate the existence of two spheres in addition to the seven planetary orbits. One, right above the sphere of Saturn, was the sphere of the fixed stars. The other, which is supposed to bear the signs of an abstract zodiac on its inner side, is the one the Brethren call the "all-encompassing sphere." It is that sphere, the ninth and ultimate of the series, which carries all the other spheres from East to West (above the Earth) in its twenty-four-hour revolution. The zodiacal band, which may be defined as the sector of the all-encompassing sphere to which the movements of the planets are confined, is divided into twelve regular portions or signs of thirty degrees each, namely Aries, Taurus, Gemini, Cancer, Leo, Virgo, Libra, Scorpio, Sagittarius, Capricorn, Aquarius, and Pisces.

With reference to the zodiac, the discourse turns to what seems to interest the Brethren more than the great principles of cosmology, namely a systematic exposition of the properties assigned to those twelve signs, the seven planets, and the innumerable kinds of combinations which the celestial motions are able to produce. What results is an amazing set of technical terms which the Brethren could have found, for a good part, in Ptolemy's *Apotelesmatika* (also known as *Tetrabiblos*). There is little point in reproducing here the details of this tangle, but a glimpse of the astrological art can be seen in the definition of a zodiacal sign as either northern or southern, male or female, diurnal or nocturnal, wet or dry, cold or warm, oriental or occidental, to give but the most common of those determinations. A sign may also be variously regarded as stable, unstable, or corporeal, or as of a fiery, earthy, airy, or watery nature. The last four adjectives are directly related to the theory of triplicities which played a major role in Muslim astrology, as we shall see in connection with the conjunctions of Saturn and Jupiter in the *Rasa'il*. Astrologers used to conceive of the zodiac as a circle in which four triangles can be inscribed, each one of them connecting three signs of the same nature. Echoing the four elements of the sub-lunar world, these triangles were called the triplicities of Fire (Aries, Leo, Sagittarius), Earth (Taurus, Virgo, Capricorn), Air (Gemini, Libra, Aquarius), and Water (Cancer, Scorpio, Pisces) respectively.

After the signs, which are compared to the "bodies" of the physical world, the authors proceed to speak of the planets (the "spirits") to which they devote another compendium of technical expressions. For the present purpose, notions such as aspect, detriment, exaltation, dejection, apogee, light, nature, or decan will give an idea of what the experts of the past – as the Brethren no doubt were – used to juggle with. With much zeal, the Brethren list in full the elements of various systems, such as the sequence of the twelve houses, as counted from the ascendant: house of life from the degree cutting the Eastern horizon (properly called the ascendant) to the thirtieth degree, house of wealth from the thirtieth to the sixtieth, and so on until one reaches the three hundred and sixtieth degree of the circle, which is the last of the houses and which is called the house of enemies. In a section about the planetary revolutions, the Brethren also give a detailed account of the twenty-eight lunar mansions, one of the few astronomical theories known to the Arabs before the rise of Islam and possibly inherited from the Indian system of *nakshatras*.

The end of Epistle 3 is particularly noteworthy in that it constitutes a kind of defense of astrology based on the emanationist scheme described in Chapter 2. The World Soul communicates its influence to the entire revolution, first to the fixed stars, then to the planets and to the four elements of the world of coming-to-be and passing-away, then finally to all the creatures composed from those elements – in other words, the mineral, vegetal, and animal kingdoms with man at the top. The influence on such individuals will be favorable if, at the moment chosen for computation, the celestial configuration proves to lie on noble and harmonious relations. In the opposite case, it will be unfavorable. In this respect, one may note the role assigned to each planet according to its own nature. Thus, the Sun is like the king, the Moon like the minister or the heir to the throne, Mercury like the secretary, Venus like the servants and the slaves,

Mars like the chief of the army, Jupiter like the judge, and Saturn like the treasurer.

The beginning of **Epistle 16** ("The heavens and the world") overlaps in part with the cosmological presentation in Epistle 3. Here too we find an explanation of the heavenly spheres, the only difference being that the Brethren now make a special effort to identify the last two spheres of the system with the Seat and the Throne of God mentioned in the Qur'an. Less banal is the argument demonstrating why there cannot be any empty space between the spheres or even outside the all-encompassing sphere, and the passage in which the Brethren identify the distances between the different spheres of the universe and the Earth in figures differing from those of Ptolemy. In what follows they deal with various other data about the starry sphere and the planetary spheres, the most important of which are listed in a table which gives, for each of these eight spheres, the measure of its movement relative to the all-encompassing sphere, the period of its sidereal revolution, and the number of revolutions it makes around the Earth during that period. As in any introduction to astronomy, the Brethren have to explain why the Moon, which has the fastest speed of revolution, can also be defined as the slowest of all planets since it is the one which seems to retrogress the most with regard to the general movement of the sphere from East to West.

It is for the general purpose of clarifying such apparent paradoxes that the Brethren tell two allegorical stories, namely that of the pilgrims circumambulating the Ka'ba and that of the seven individuals revolving at different speeds around a circular city. The text reveals, as we have already stressed, that the Brethren's primary aim here was to illustrate the Great Year as a general conjunction of planets taking place in the first degree of Aries and coinciding with what the Brethren themselves call the "great resurrection" (*al-qiyama al-kubra*). After explaining the most patent of planetary conjunctions, that is, the solar and lunar eclipses, the Brethren return to the great resurrection in order to conclude the epistle with one of their most beloved analogies. The great resurrection will mark the end of the universe, when the World Soul will leave the world, just as the "small resurrection" – for which the Brethren invite their readers to prepare – will take place at the moment when the individual soul is freed from its jail by the death of the body.

Epistle 36 ("Revolutions and cycles") can be subdivided into two major parts. In the first the Brethren list a number of astronomical periods. In the second, considerably longer, they trace the influence of those periods on the world of coming-to-be and passing-away. In the first part, they set about to define – or rather affirm – the existence of no less than five species of revolutions and six genera (or 120 species) of conjunctions, to which they add, without further explanation, four "millennial" periods: 7,000 years, 12,000 years, 51,000 years, and 360,000 years. They identify the longest revolution as that which is completed, once in 360,000 years, by the starry sphere on the zodiac – a clear reference to the movement of precession with its Ptolemaic value. The shortest revolution is the diurnal movement from East to West, with its period of a mere twenty-four hours. The longest period of conjunction is that of the seven planets in the first degree of Aries, taking place once every 360,000 years and coinciding with "one day of the days of the Macrocosm" according to the Indian *Zij al-Sindhind*. The shortest period of conjunction is that of the Moon, once a month, with each one of the other planets.

The Brethren proceed to give a few examples of revolutions and conjunctions in between these extremes, among others the three famous types of conjunctions between Jupiter and Saturn. The basis of this theory is that the point where the two superior planets meet every twenty years, is not fixed once and for all, but slowly shifts around the zodiacal band with the effect that it will pass to a sign of another triplicity after around 240 years (that is, twelve conjunctions), and will eventually come back to a sign of the same triplicity as the first one after around 960 years (or forty-eight conjunctions). This theory was first formulated by Sasanid astrologers and had enjoyed considerable fame ever since, the Brethren being among its admirers, as will be shown in greater detail below.

The second part of the epistle reconsiders all these periods from the point of view of their effects on the sub-lunar world. The examples of portentous revolutions are far too numerous – and too repetitive – for all of them to be mentioned here. The whole spectrum of astrological influences ranges from the coming-to-be of worms, bugs, and lice owing to the diurnal movement of the all-encompassing sphere, to interchanges between seas and continents on the Earth's surface as a consequence of the equinoctial precession. Particular mention is made of the yearly cycle of the seasons, the most remarkable period in nature and the model of all, as it were, with its fourfold sequence of birth, maturity, decay, and death.

Another important section is that in which the Brethren seek to explain how the revolution of a given sphere affects the length of gestation and the lifespan of a given species at the same time. The account is somewhat unclear on the subject of the conjunctions and the millennial periods, which it discusses in the middle of a general survey of the seven "species of things from which astrologers seek to draw indications" (*R.* III, 266). But along with other predictions of a different nature, the Brethren refer here to the effects of the three main types of Saturn–Jupiter conjunctions. In agreement with the traditional doctrine, they identify the shortest period (twenty years) as the one instigating changes of individuals on the royal throne, the medium period (240 years) as inducing the shift of dynasties from one nation to the next, and the longest period (960 years, often rounded to a millennium) as the one bringing about changes of empires and religious confessions. The epistle concludes with the important comment that a period can be influenced by a favorable or unfavorable conjunction.

THE THEORY OF PROPHETIC CYCLES

As mentioned already, the *Rasa'il* contain many other passages of an astronomical or astrological nature, but these mostly repeat what is said in Epistles 3, 16, and 36, so there is no need to examine them in detail. They share a strongly determinist theorization of the world and its evolution. We are indebted to Yves Marquet for having undertaken to reconstitute a coherent system from the indescribable disorder of data scattered throughout the 52 (or 51) epistles and the "Comprehensive Epistle," many of them taking the form of subtle references, and above all for having drawn attention to one particular aspect of this astral determinism, which he called the theory of prophetic cycles, and which plays a role of paramount importance in the Brethren's scheme of things.

The Brethren do not really explain this theory of prophetic cycles, but rather allude to it time and again. It seems to rest on a fusion of two earlier assumptions. One is that planetary conjunctions influence the course of history, above all when they involve the two superior planets, as mentioned above. This was one of the basic ideas behind the most common practices of Persian and Arabic astrology, and the Brethren could have derived it directly from the "Book of Religions and Dynasties" (*Kitab al-milal wa-l-duwal*) by the famous Abu Ma'shar (d. 886), where an impressive series of examples of such conjunctions and their influences are listed. The other assumption is that world history as a whole is cyclical and that each cycle is itself divided into seven prophetic eras. According to this scheme, which the Brethren share with a great number of Shi'ite – especially Ismaili – authors from about the same time, the first six prophets to have inaugurated eras in the present cycle are Adam, Noah, Abraham, Moses, Jesus, and Muhammad, the prophet of Islam. In the Ismaili version, each "prophet" (*nabi*) has brought a "revealed law" (*shari'a*) to replace that of his predecessor, and each is a "speaker" (*natiq*) whose mission is to provide his own people with the "exoteric form" (*zahir*) of the divine revelation. Each one of these prophets is succeeded by a "legatee" (*wasi*), who was in charge of disclosing to a chosen few the "esoteric form" (*batin*) of that particular revelation. The legatee of the Muslim era is 'Ali b. Abi Talib, the cousin and son-in-law of Muhammad and the first *imam* (literally, "the leader") of the Islamic community according to most Shi'ites. Only with the seventh and last prophet will the inner and external meaning of the entire Revelation become open and manifest to the whole of mankind. This seventh and last imam is known as the *mahdi* (literally, "the rightly-guided") or the *qa'im* (literally, "the one who stands up"). His coming will equal the coming of the *qiyama* ("resurrection"). For the time being, the esoteric secrets of Revelation will remain the property of a succession of imams (and a chosen few outstanding people such as the Brethren themselves) who will transmit them clandestinely so as to keep themselves and the message protected from the perversity of this world.

In itself, this scheme does not have anything to do with astrology. At the hands of the Brethren, however, it is endowed with two remarkable characteristics that radically modify it. In the first place, the seven eras are all assigned an equal length of a thousand years, so that the sum total of one cycle of history is seven thousand years – a figure in which one can recognize one of the "millennial" periods described in Epistle 36. Second, each one of these "thousands" is said to correspond with one of the seven planets. This is astrology at its best, with its ability to suggest unseen relationships and thought-provoking networks of combinations. For there is, as will be seen, much more than simple playfulness or curiosity behind the association of, say, the planet Mercury with Islam or Venus with Christianity, let alone that between the Moon and the messianic era of the *qa'im* inaugurating the resurrection.

THE ORIGIN OF PROPHETIC ASTROLOGY

Where do the elements of that prophetic astrology come from? Sasanid Persia knew of "millennial" periods, notably a twelve-thousand-year cycle in which each zodiacal sign exerted predominant influence in one millennium. That sort of chronology could have been introduced to the Muslims as early as the eighth century CE via such specialists as Masha'allah. A Persian Jew from Basra, Masha'allah was active at the time when the great Mansur (r. 754–775), the second Abbasid caliph, was founding Baghdad. The conception of millennial periods associated with planets is found in the Hermetic *Kitab al-Ustutas*, which the Brethren knew and even quoted from. That their own theory of prophetic cycles may have been inspired by the *Kitab al-Ustutas* is all the more probable since, as was shown by Marquet, the treatise already contains the idea of a corresponding series of wise men bringing a new and better wisdom to mankind. But they may also have been influenced by the *Poimandres*, for this part of the famous Hellenistic *Corpus Hermeticum* also includes an account of the seven men corresponding to the natures of the seven planets, as will be shown further in Chapter 5. As for the "Ismaili" slicing of the cycle according to the six-plus-one motif, we may assert with confidence that it was greatly facilitated in Islam by the Qur'an, which echoes the biblical Genesis in stating: "God, Who created the Heavens and the Earth in six Days, then settled Himself on the Throne" (Q. 2:54 and 32:4). One could invoke the authority of the Qur'an even for the idea of assigning a thousand years to each era, since the Holy Book of Islam, this time in accord with the Psalms, says in one place: "Verily, a day in the sight of thy Lord is like a thousand years of your reckoning" (Q. 22:47). As one would expect, the Brethren did not miss this opportunity to have the Qur'an on their side and duly quoted the verse in their *Rasa'il*, more particularly in Epistle 40 ("On causes and effects").

Once an astrological, planetary significance had been attached to the theory of prophetic millennia, one would imagine that writers as syncretic by bent as the Brethren found it hard to resist the temptation to go a step further and identify each prophetic millennium with a Saturn–Jupiter conjunction of the longest type, namely, when the conjunction of the two planets comes back to a sign of the same nature as in the beginning. As mentioned before, these conjunctions are meant to indicate the changes of religious confessions (*milal*) and empires (*duwal*), and they occur every 960 solar years, which seems to be an acceptable approximation to a millennium. When they are converted into lunar years, as those using the Islamic moon-based calendar would find it natural to do, the approximation is even better, for 960 solar years is equivalent to about 990 lunar years. The Brethren implicitly acknowledge this in Epistle 36, where they refer to the longest type of Saturn–Jupiter conjunctions as taking place "once every 1,000 years approximately" (*R.* III, 266).

A PROPITIOUS CONJUNCTION IN SIGHT

On the basis of this theory the Brethren inferred that something momentous was about to happen. There would be a "recommencement of the revolution of revealing and awakening, as well as of dissipation of worries for mankind," they tell their potential supporters in the snippet quoted at the beginning of this chapter, and this event would result "from the transfer of the conjunction, from the sign of fiery triplicities to the sign of vegetal and animal triplicities, in the tenth circle which corresponds to the house of power and the appearance of the eminent people." In a now famous article published back in 1915, Paul Casanova tried to date the *Rasa'il* based on the astronomical and astrological contents of this passage. Assuming on secure grounds that the transfer of conjunction alluded to in Epistle 48 ("The modalities of the call to go to God") could only be that of Saturn and Jupiter from a fiery to an earthy sign, he looked for confirmation of the event in the astronomical tables available to him and found that such a transfer took place on 19 November 1047, according to the Julian calendar. Since he was convinced of the Brethren's affiliation to Ismailism, and more particularly to the Fatimid branch of it, he read the passage as "an obvious allusion to the expected triumph of the Fatimids," or in other words their anticipated conquest of Iraq, as well as a remarkable prediction of that triumph, for although the Fatimids did not actually conquer Iraq, either in 1047 or later, a *khutba* (public sermon on the occasion of the Friday prayer) given in Baghdad in 1059 did mention the Fatimid caliph Mustansir (r. 1036–1094) as the sovereign (for reasons to do with rivalry between rival potentates in the area at the time). Consequently, Casanova dated the writing of the *Rasa'il Ikhwan al-Safa'* to some time before that fatal conjunction, suggesting as the most probable period the twenty-year span which separates it from the previous Saturn–Jupiter conjunction in 1027.

In its very rigidity, this interpretation lays itself open to criticism and it was spurned as "clearly erroneous" by Marquet, who for his part chose to view the same passage as alluding, not to that final victory of the Fatimid movement, but rather to a preliminary success such as the conquest of Egypt in 969, or even the proclamation in 909 of 'Ubayd Allah al-Mahdi (r. 909–934), first caliph of the Fatimid dynasty in North Africa. It remains a fact, none the less, that Casanova's astronomical demonstration is fundamentally right and that his interpretation, unlike any of Marquet's, is faithfully based on the indications contained in the passage. For 1047 is the only year in which the Saturn–Jupiter conjunction can reasonably be said to have changed from a fiery sign (Sagittarius) to an earthy one (Capricorn). The phenomenon occurs, let us remember, only once every thousand (lunar) years approximately, so that we should have to go to either the first century CE or the present epoch to find other examples. Before 1047, as one can easily calculate from modern computerized tables, the only significant transfers are those from a watery (Scorpio) to a fiery (Sagittarius) sign in 809 and from an airy (Libra) to a watery (Scorpio) sign in 571 CE. In the eye of Muslim astrologers, this network of dates was anything but innocent or meaningless. For in famous treatises of historical astrology such as those compiled by Abu Ma'shar and Masha'allah it was already common practice to identify the conjunction of 571 as the one which had indicated, or even determined, the birth of Muhammad, the prophet of Islam. In other words, by alluding to the imminent transfer of the conjunction, the Brethren suggest to those able to understand that the first half of the millennium inaugurated by Muhammad was now about to reach its end and that a grand renewal was to inaugurate a new era in the not too distant future.

The Brethren do not tell us exactly how they envisaged that renewal. Contrary to what Casanova and Marquet believed, it is unlikely that they were adherents of the Fatimids or that they hoped for a great conquest in the fateful year, but they certainly expected the change of the Saturn–Jupiter conjunction to transfer sovereignty from one nation to another. In other words, they could expect power to move from Muhammad's people, the Arabs (who still supplied the caliphs) to some non-Arab people, in all likelihood the Persians, and they probably expected this change of regime to lead to general acceptance of their own philosophical ideas. Thereafter, there would only be another half millennium left before the appearance of the *qa'im* of the resurrection.

How long before the first of these two auspicious events were the Brethren writing? They sensibly refrain from saying so explicitly. A few lines after the passage cited, they merely state that the moment "is not far away" (*R.* IV, 146). Later in Epistle 48, referring to the conjunction again, they simply stress the convergence of views among the Brethren, who all assert "that there will soon be a wonderful event, propitious to religion and to the life of this world as well, namely the renewal of royalty in the kingdom, and the transfer of the empire from one nation to another, and that there are evident indications and clear signs of this" (*R.* IV, 190). This is too vague a prediction to identify the time of writing with any accuracy. Casanova opted for the years before 1047, as we have seen, but a much earlier date would be equally acceptable, given the wider system of prophetic history developed by the Brethren.

THE SLEEPERS OF THE CAVE

The Brethren also reveal their aspirations in the eschatological fable that came to be known in both eastern and western Christianity as the Legend of the Seven Sleepers of Ephesus. The myth is Christian in origin and has been shown to date back to the time of Bishop Stephen of Ephesus in the middle of the fifth century CE. It tells how a group of companions escaped from a Roman emperor's persecutions by taking refuge in a cave, where they fell asleep, only to realize when they woke up that their slumber had lasted for several hundred years. This legend developed in countless different directions and the record of its transformations and adaptations, inside or outside the Christian sphere, fills entire volumes. Within the Muslim world, the story is of particular significance, since it is found, with the necessary changes of perspective, in the Qur'an itself. *Sura* 18:9–26 tells of those who "stayed in their Cave for three hundred years, and nine more," and about whose precise number one could only conjecture:

> (Some) say they were three, the dog being the fourth among them; (others) say they were five, the dog being the sixth, – doubtfully guessing at the unknown; (yet others) say they were seven, the dog being the eighth. Say: "My Lord knows best their number; it is but few that know (the facts about) them". Enter not, therefore, into controversies concerning them, except on a matter that is clear, nor consult any of them about (the affair) of the Sleepers.

Generation after generation, the best experts in Muslim exegesis did their utmost to compare this canonical version of the story with extra-Qur'anic accounts in the hope of finding explanations for such problems as the number of sleepers, the duration of their sleeping period and the role of the accompanying dog. At a more popular level, the story of the Cave inspired ever-growing feelings of devotion to and sympathy for the figures of the sleepers.

The Brethren's elaboration of the legend does not seem so far to have attracted the attention it deserves. They deal with it at the end of Epistle 38, devoted to "Rebirth and resurrection." There (*R.* III, 315–320), they tell the story of a king who was granted seven sons in as many "days" of a "week" due to end with a "Friday", here to be understood as an allegory for the day of resurrection. Each of the sons was entrusted with part of the father's kingdom and advised to govern his people well. But the first son, who is presented as inattentive and absent-minded, was seduced by an envious advisor into seeking

> what it was not appropriate for him to obtain before the appropriate time or to request before it was due. He became conscious of his sexual organs and aware of his sin, so he fled for fear of his father, going about in his kingdom as if in concealment. He experienced distress, misery, and adversity, and endured hardship and misfortune. One day, he remembered the way he had lived in his father's favor and grieved over his loss, weeping with regret. Then he felt drowsy and fell asleep. He was brought to his father, who said: "Let him sleep until Friday."

Evidently, the eldest son is Adam. The story goes on to deal similarly with the next sons, from the second to the sixth, who are easily recognized as Noah, Abraham, Moses, Jesus, and Muhammad. In other words, the seven sons stand for the seven prophets of the cycle. But each son is also said to possess character traits corresponding to a planet. The Brethren explicitly say so only in the case of the five middle sons – who are connected with Saturn, Jupiter, Mars, Venus, and Mercury – but the text is clear enough to show that the same is true of the first and the last, whose connection is with the Sun and the Moon respectively. Once the identification of the sons with the seven prophets and their millennia is admitted, the sequence is as follows: Adam – Sun, Noah – Saturn, Abraham – Jupiter, Moses – Mars, Jesus – Venus, Muhammad – Mercury, *Qa'im* of resurrection – Moon.

Although relatively long, the section concerning the sixth and penultimate day of the week, i.e. Muhammad's, deserves to be quoted in full, for it is evidently the one of the greatest importance for the myth as a whole. The text reads:

> Then on the sixth day their father said to the celestial bodies: "Choose a day for my son who looks like Mercury so that he may descend to the world of coming-to-be and passing-away, wake up his sleeping brothers and call them to his truth, for I am satisfied with them (i.e. I have forgiven them). Let him order them to prepare for prayer. Tomorrow is the feast, Friday, so the judges will appear. Let him give judgement among them about the things they disagreed on". The masters of the celestial bodies and the leaders of the stars gathered in the house of Mars and took counsel together. The leader of the stars and their king, the Sun, said: "From my power and highest virtues I choose to give him leadership, sovereignty, power, elevated status, splendor, magnificence, praise, glorification, offering and gifts". The oldest of them, Saturn, said: "From my power I choose to give him clemency, dignity, patience, constancy, insight, high-mindedness, attentiveness, trustworthiness, thought and deliberation". Jupiter, the just judge, said: "From my power I choose to provide him with religion, scrupulous observance, goodness, integrity, equity, justice, truth, correctness, truthfulness, fidelity, safeguarding and manliness". Mars, the master of the armies, said: "From my power and virtues I choose to provide him with determination, sharpness, bravery, courage, ardour, fearlessness, triumph, victory, granting, munificence

> and wakefulness". Venus, the sister of the celestial bodies, said: "From my power and virtues I choose to provide him with good looks, beauty, wholeness, perfection, compassion, mercy, finery, neatness, love, affection, joy and pleasure". The youngest brother, the least conspicuous of them in appearance, yet the most illustrious of them (the one whose skill is the most apparent, whose sciences are the most numerous, whose wonders are the most widely known and the most brilliant), Mercury, said: "From my power, virtues and praiseworthy characteristics I choose to provide and strengthen him with eloquence, fine diction, discernment, astuteness, insight, sophistication, recitation, chant, and the sciences and wisdom". The mother of celestial bodies, namely the Moon, said: "I will nurse him and make him grow. From my power and virtues I provide him with light, brilliance, increase, growth, movement in the three regions, shifting in travels, fulfilment of hopes, knowledge of past lives and events, and the science of appointed times". Then the spheres turned around, the powers of the spiritual beings shook violently, and the people of the heavens rejoiced. During the night of Destiny, before the rising dawn, the master of Resurrection came down to the world of coming-to-be, to blow the trumpet (*R.* III, 317–318).

All this, which reminds us of motifs used in fairy-tales, refers to the exceptional configuration of the heavens – a conjunction of all planets, including Saturn and Jupiter, in the house of Mars – that ruled over the coming-to-be of the last and most illustrious of all prophets up to now. In confirmation of the view that this prophet is Muhammad it may be said that the house of Mars is most probably to be identified with Scorpio, which Muslim astrologers traditionally recognized as the "indicator" or "significator" (*dalil*) of the Arabs. The reader's immediate reaction will probably be that the story develops quite differently from Muhammad's, but as the following lines clearly show, the baby is not meant to be Muhammad alone; rather, it stands for both him and the message he was chosen to convey, and it is the message – the true religion of Islam – that falls asleep in the cave:

> This baby stayed in the womb for forty of the days of the Sun, and was suckled for twenty days, until he had grown up, developed, reached full maturity and flourished. He resembled his third brother

> more than anyone else, for he looked like Mercury, who is the brother of Jupiter, because of the opposition between them, their quadrature and the opposition of their spheres. This baby grew into the most perfect of all the brothers in body and form, and he was a cultured man of letters, a learned sage, a mighty king, a just imam, and a messenger-prophet. His father entrusted him with his kingdom and that of his brothers in their entirety. So he came forth and subjugated whoever opposed him while elevating and empowering those who agreed with him, and ruled his kingdom for around thirty of the days of Sun. Then he thought highly of himself and the evil eye fell upon him, so he fell sick and remained in his bed for around a thousand of the days of the Moon, ill in body and sick in soul. Then he left for another abode. He got up a little, walked and became stronger, got lively and happy, and drank from the love of this world, its illusions and longings. So he got drunk from the wine of his passions and entered his father's cave, where he fell asleep along with his brothers. They remained there for a long time (*R.* III, 318–319).

As Marquet rightly noted, the "forty days" of gestation and the "twenty days" of suckling correspond to the pre-revelation and revelation periods in the prophet's life, for he is supposed to have been forty years old when he received his first revelation and to have spent ten years as a prophet in Mecca before moving to Medina, where he spent the last ten years of his life. The approximately thirty solar years during which the young prince rules his kingdom are clearly to be identified with the epoch of rightly-guided caliphs (*rashidun*), namely the first four caliphs of Islam up to 'Ali's time. The evil eye striking the baby because it thought too highly of itself is, I would assume, an allusion to the Battle of Siffin in 657 when, as the Shi'ites saw it, the rightly-guided 'Ali was challenged by an arrogant rival called Mu'awiya. This was the first major dissension within Islam and, as a consequence of it, 'Ali would progressively lose his leadership over the whole community. The few years of 'Ali's caliphate – until 661 – are also perfectly rendered, with the observation that the sixth brother "fell sick and remained in his bed for around a thousand of the days of the Moon, ill in the body and sick in the soul." For since a day of the Moon is surely to be understood as a day in the proper sense, we find that a thousand of these days corresponds with three years. As for the phrase "Then he left for another abode," I cannot think of it as referring to anything more suitable than the transfer of power to Damascus, the new capital of the Umayyad dynasty inaugurated by Mu'awiya in the same year.

The end of the fable deserves to be quoted as well, for it contains one last numeric indication of great significance, as a signal of the ultimate meaning of the story, for the Brethren now tell us how long the six remained asleep in the Cave before being woken from the slumber of negligence:

> When the era of slumber came to an end and the appointed time approached, their father called them: "Is it not about time for you to awaken from your sleep and be aroused from your negligence, to remember what you have forgotten regarding your origin, and come back from your journeys to your place of return? Indeed, for every beginning there is an end, for every life an annihilation and for every death and sleeper an awakening. Hasten from your exile to your place of return. For the creation of the seven heavens was completed in six days, and tomorrow, Friday, your Lord will sit on the throne which will be borne on that day by eight (angels)". So the brothers – of whom it is said that they were seven and that the eighth one was their dog – awoke, after a torpor of 354 of the days of the Sun according to the computation of the Moon. They conferred together about how long they had stayed in their cave. Their father said to their brother: *Enter not, therefore, into controversies concerning them, except on a matter that is clear, nor consult any of them about [the affair] of the sleepers* (Q. 18:22). So they hid and concealed their secrets, for *there is no confidential talk between three where He is not the fourth, nor between five where He is not the sixth, nor between fewer or more where He is not with them, wherever they may be. Then, on the day of resurrection, He will tell them what they have done* (Q. 58:7). O brother, understand these allusions and these instructions, judge their likes on analogy with them, and do not disclose the secrets, so that maybe you too will awaken from the sleep of negligence and slumber of ignorance before the trumpet is blown and the herald calls to prayer on Friday – *Hasten to the remembrance of God and leave off business. That is best for you* (Q. 62:9) – and before the sinners are driven off in droves to Hell (*R.* III, 319–320).

Whereas the Qur'an mentions that the companions "stayed in their Cave for three hundred years, and nine more" (Q. 18:25), the Brethren speak of "a torpor of 354 of the days of the Sun according to the computation of the Moon." There has always been fair agreement among the exegetes that the 309 years of the Holy Book are lunar and equal to 300 solar years. That the 354 years of the Brethren are also lunar is clear, but why do they depart from the figure given in the Qur'an?

CONCEALMENT AND MANIFESTATION

Proceeding on the assumption that the text is not corrupt, the forty-five (lunar) years by which the Ikhwan differ may, I think, be explained as follows. Unlike the Qur'anic figure of 309, that of 354 gains a clear symbolic resonance from the astronomical context in which it is located, since it is said to be a "year of years," exactly as a period of 365 years would be in a solar computation. So let us take the Brethren at their word and bring the elements of the story as they relate it, that is, "on analogy with their likes." 19 November 1047 is, as we have seen, the only possible date for the famous transfer of the conjunction alluded to in Epistle 48. This corresponds to 28 Jumada I of the year 439 in the Muslim calendar. If we subtract the 354 years mentioned in the story from that date, we find that the long period of sleep began in AH 85. We only need to put this result in relation to some other momentous dates in early Islamic history to understand that it fits well with the chronology of events as generally received, even more so when one adopts the traditionally Shi'ite point of view (see chart, p. xvii). Thus, Muhammad had died in AH 10 (632 CE) and the Battle of Siffin had taken place in AH 36 (657 CE), leaving an enormous trauma for all those who were partisans of 'Ali and who would later be defined as forming the Shi'ite branch. This state of distress became more complete and effective still when, as is well known, Husayn, 'Ali's younger son and the third imam of the community, was assassinated with many of his men at Karbala' (Iraq), by the army of Yazid b. Mu'awiya, the second Umayyad caliph. The disaster of Karbala', from which the Shi'ite collective consciousness started to develop its distinctive apology of martyrdom, occurred in AH 61 (681 CE). In AH 85 (704 CE), only a quarter of century later, the fourth imam, 'Ali b. Husayn – better known as Zayn al-'Abidin ("the Ornament of the Worshipers") for his extreme piety – was clearly not in a position to challenge the uncompromising regime of 'Abd al-Malik (r. 685–705). Rather, classical sources agree in reporting that Husayn's son and successor abandoned command of the resistance to others and dedicated himself to a life made up entirely of prayer and mourning. It is an epoch in which many Shi'ite intellectuals, especially those who rejected any kind of violence, may well have lost their last hope of assuming a leading political role. What all these idealists were constrained to do was just wait for better circumstances to return.

THE RISING OF THE THREE QA'IMS

The *Rasa'il* provide us with other indications that the authors placed the beginning of the sleeping period – in other words, the start of concealment of the vision of Islam as they portrayed it – in the Karbala' disaster, or perhaps just in its immediate aftermath, but certainly not a half-century later, as the unemended Qur'anic figure would have required. One of these indications is implicit – it is the complete absence, throughout the Epistles, of any name of Umayyad caliphs after Yazid b. Mu'awiya (r. 680–683), as though the entire period after him had been written off. But there is explicit evidence as well, such as this passage from Epistle 44 on "those who surrendered their bodies to death on the day of Karbala', refusing to acknowledge the rule of Yazid and Ziyad and enduring thirst, calumniation and beating until their souls departed from their bodies and were raised to the kingdom of the heaven, where they met their pure ancestors: Muhammad, 'Ali, the Emigrants and the Helpers who had followed them in the hard times" (*R.* IV, 33). Yet the clearest confirmation comes from Epistle 50 ("The species of governance"), in which we find the assertion that the Karbala' tragedy and the misfortunes inflicted on the family of the Prophet were "the cause of the concealment of the Brethren of Purity and of the period of dominion of the Friends of the Loyalty, (which will continue) until God allows the rising (*qiyam*) of the first, the second and the third of them at times when it will be appropriate for them to rise, when they will come into view from their cave and wake up from their long sleep" (*R.* IV, 269).

How are we meant to understand this notion of three different *qa'ims* rising in succession, when there has so far only been talk of one *qa'im*, namely the one expected at the end of the cycle in the general scheme of millennial prophetic cycles? The Brethren do not tell us, so that again we are reduced to conjectures. I would nevertheless assume that there is a way out of the puzzle, but for this we need first to sum up some of the results we have obtained thus far. Of paramount importance is the need to distinguish carefully between, on the one hand, the propitious Saturn–Jupiter conjunction predicted by the Brethren as a fairly close event and, on the other hand, that other Saturn–Jupiter conjunction, not referred to as such in the text but which in virtue of the theory must coincide with the appearance of the *qa'im* of the resurrection. Technically speaking, the former is one of those "medium conjunctions" which take place about every 240 years, as we have seen, and which are believed to coincide with shifts of sovereignty from one nation or dynasty to the next. By contrast, the latter belongs to the category of "longest conjunctions," that is, conjunctions which take place every 960 years or so and are supposed to coincide with the changes of empires and religious confessions. We have found that the "medium conjunction" heralded by the Brethren in Epistle 48 – let us call it the "imminent conjunction" – is the one located midway through the sixth millennium. This means that it is in fact the second of the three "medium conjunctions" that are intercalated between the two "longest conjunctions" at the beginning and the end of the "Islamic millennium," as follows:

- 571 CE: "longest conjunction" (from Libra to Scorpio): birth of Muhammad.
- 809 CE: first "medium conjunction" (from Scorpio to Sagittarius).
- 1047 CE: second "medium conjunction" (from Sagittarius to Capricorn); this is the "imminent conjunction" of the Ikhwan.
- 1286 CE: third "medium conjunction" (from Capricorn to Aquarius).
- 1524 CE: "longest conjunction" (from Aquarius to Libra); this corresponds to the rising of the *qa'im* of the resurrection.

Now let us project ourselves back to the time the Brethren lived, and try to imagine how they could have made use of this kind of calendar. Looking backward was not very stimulating, as it only made plain that the "true religion of Islam" had for long been forced to enter a period of concealment. When did this period begin? The Brethren were free to speculate, and indeed they did, as we have seen, by choosing the time of Karbala' or the years immediately afterwards as the starting point of the period. Could the theory of Saturn–Jupiter conjunctions be adduced to justify this choice? This is most unlikely, for the Brethren must have noticed at once that they could not make anything out of 809 CE, that is, the year of the first "medium conjunction." At the same time, what they could not have failed to notice either is that the same theory could very fittingly serve their own vision of the future. The end of the sleeping period was near at hand. This they could take for granted from the "imminent conjunction" due to take place in 1047 CE. But important though this event might be in terms of dynastic changes, this would only be like a first step in the longer process towards full manifestation. For the second step one would have to wait for the next "medium conjunction," the last one of those implying local changes of nations or dynasties. The third and final step, in other words the full manifestation of the Brethren's cause, would come at the end of the millennium itself, with the universal upheaval resulting from the "longest conjunction."

Would it be so absurd to interpret the reference to the three successive *qa'ims* in Epistle 50 along the same lines? I think not, for this is also what the very context of the passage would seem to invite us to understand. There, indeed, the Brethren embark on a strange analogy which leads them to put side by side three yearly calendars, each one said to contain four "days of feast" more or less in agreement with the seasons. The first type, which the Brethren term the "Greek" or "philosophical" calendar but which they may plausibly have drawn from Harran (as Marquet suggests), has its four feasts regularly distributed around the year, since they are said to correspond to the spring equinox, the summer solstice, the autumn equinox, and the winter solstice. The second type is presented as the "Islamic" or "legal" calendar. Interestingly enough, its four "days of feast" are said to be the *'id al-fitr* (the breaking of the fast at the end of the month of Ramadan), the *'id al-adha* (the sacrifice at the end of the pilgrimage period), the *'id ghadir Khumm* (a decisively Shi'ite feast in memory of the day the Prophet is reported to have introduced 'Ali as the *mawla* or master of the believers), and finally the "sad feast" in which the prophet Muhammad's death is celebrated. Yet surely the most intriguing section of the passage is the one that follows. In it (*R.* IV, 269–270), the authors allude to the four "feasts of the Brethren," in other words a more esoteric system of their own which they view as a synthesis of the "philosophic" and the "Islamic" calendars. The text is cryptic in places, as one might have expected. What nevertheless clearly appears is that the authors stress the distinction between, on the one hand, the "sad" period of concealment inside the Cave – in which they say they find themselves for the time being – and, on the other hand, those three happier periods which make up the rest of the cycle and which they identify in turn with the "way out (of the Cave) (*khuruj*) of the first *qa'im,*" "the rising (*qiyam*) of the second *qa'im,*" and "the rising of the third *qa'im.*"

It is time to conclude the present investigation. There would no doubt be a lot to learn from a closer comparison of the Brethren's doctrine of prophetic cycles with similar predictions found elsewhere in Arabic literature. Thus, the Byzantine astrologer Theophilus, who lived in the time of the Umayyads, predicted that Islam would last

960 years, since this is the period required for the Saturn–Jupiter conjunction to take place again in the sign of Scorpio, as it had done at the rising of Islam. This report we owe to the historian Ibn Khaldun (d. 1406) who lists in his famous "Introduction" (*Muqaddima*) other astrological predictions about the end of Islam, including by such great Muslim authorities as Abu Ma'shar or Ya'qub b. Ishaq al-Kindi. There is little hope, however, that the comparison of all this material would enable us to get a perfectly coherent picture of the Brethren's theory. After all, astrology is one of those arts whose subtlety may easily lead a scholar to doubt his own ability to understand. "God knows better," as both Ibn Khaldun and the Brethren would have said.

4

ENCYCLOPAEDISM

> We have produced an epistle for each branch of the above-mentioned sciences and mentioned in them some of those meanings, and we have completed them with a general epistle to awaken the negligent and guide the beginners, excite the interest of students and serve as a path for those who learn. Be happy by means of it, my brother, and show this epistle to your brethren and friends; make them desirous of science, urge them to renounce this world, and show them the way to the last abode! (*R.* I, 274)

The titles of the Epistles reproduced at the end of Chapter 1 convey a general idea of the scope of the work and the order of the disciplines. The scope is clearly encyclopaedic, although fields of knowledge as significant as medicine or history are nowhere to be found in the list. As for the inner organization of the system, it seems at first sight to follow a rational sequence, but it is not always as self-explanatory as one might expect. Why, for instance, does the epistle on the difference of languages (Epistle 31) form part of the second section, on the "corporeal and natural sciences"? And what is the purpose of placing the epistle on magic and the evil eye (Epistle 52) in the last section, on "nomic, divine and legal sciences"?

THE CLASSIFICATION OF KNOWLEDGE

One may reasonably hope to find answers to such questions in the text itself, for with its "Table of Contents" at the beginning and its

"Comprehensive Epistle" at the end, it is clear that a great deal of effort has gone into its organization. We also find that the Brethren have dedicated a large portion of one epistle to the classification of the sciences. I refer here to Epistle 7 ("The scientific arts and their object"), from which the above quotation is taken. After considering the purpose of science and the nine categories of scientific interrogations (Is it?, What is it?, How much is it?, How is it?, Which one is it?, Where is it?, When is it?, Why is it?, Who is it?), the Brethren devote the second half of the epistle to an account of "the types of science and their subdivisions, so as to direct the seekers of knowledge to their aims and guide them to their objectives. For the wishes of souls for different sciences and branches of culture are like the desires of bodies for foods that differ in taste, colour and smell" (*R.* I, 266). In other words, the Brethren are going to present an account of how the sciences are structured in order to help their readers find the particular science they want. Their formulation is such that on first reading, one might be forgiven for expecting them merely to present some literary pleasantries along the lines of the "Epistle on the Sciences" (*Risala fi-l-'ulum)* from our by now familiar Abu Hayyan al-Tawhidi, namely a piece of *adab* (roughly, "*belles-lettres*"), which is neither a systematic nor an exhaustive enumeration of sciences. But what comes next clearly demonstrates that the Brethren had a well-organized construction in mind. The main structure is tripartite:

> Know, my brother, that there are three kinds of sciences with which people busy themselves, namely: the propaedeutic [that is, introductory] sciences, the sciences pertaining to revealed law and the sciences of true philosophy.
>
> The propaedeutic (sciences) are those concerning the proper rules established, for the most part, for the pursuit of livelihoods and the improvement of life in this world. They are of nine kinds: (1) writing and reading; (2) language and grammar; (3) calculation and operations; (4) poetry and prosody; (5) auguries and auspices, and the like; (6) magic, talismans, alchemy, mechanical devices and the like; (7) professions and crafts; (8) sale and purchase, trades, cultivation and breeding; (9) the study of campaigns and history.

> The types of religious sciences established for the healing of souls and the pursuit of the hereafter are of six kinds: (1) the science of revelation; (2) the science of interpretation (*ta'wil*); (3) the science to do with transmissions and reports (from past religious authorities); (4) the science of jurisprudence, norms and laws; (5) the science relating to remembrance, exhortations, asceticism and mysticism; (6) the science of the interpretation of dreams. The learned in the science of revelation are those who recite the Qur'an and know it by heart. The learned in the science of interpretation are the imams and the successors of the prophets. Those who know about transmissions are the specialists of the Tradition. Those who know about the laws and norms are the jurists. Those who know about remembrance and exhortations are the worshippers, the ascetics, the monks and the like. The learned in the interpretation of dreams are the dream interpreters.
>
> The philosophical sciences are of four kinds: (1) mathematical; (2) logical; (3) physical; (4) divine. (*R*. I, 266-267)

Further divisions of the philosophical sciences will be discussed below.

PROPAEDEUTIC SCIENCES

For the moment we may stop to note that in the first place come the branches of human knowledge which the Brethren call the "propaedeutic" or "disciplinary" sciences (*al-'ulum al-riyadiyya*) and which they define as aimed first and foremost at practical affairs. These sciences teach people the rules or ways (*adab*) of pursuing their livelihood and improving their lives in this world. The Brethren do not look down upon these sciences, which they regard as useful for the terrestrial accomplishment of mankind, but they obviously see them as inferior to the sciences of the two other groups, whose purpose is not restricted to the life here below.

The Brethren were not the first to speak of propaedeutic sciences, or sciences of training. In his *Epistle on the Number of Books by Aristotle*, Kindi (d. c. 870) used exactly the same words, yet under his pen the expression unambiguously referred to the four mathematical sciences that make up the Pythagorean *quadrivium*, namely arithmetic, geometry, astronomy, and music. These four sciences, which figure prominently in Graeco-Roman education from as early as Plato onwards, were endorsed as prerequisite for other studies by scholars such as Nicomachus of Gerasa (fl. between 50 CE and 150 CE), Boethius (d. 524 CE), and Isidore of Seville (d. 636 CE), who came to be regarded as great authorities in the Latin West. The *quadrivium* thus became a standard feature of education in Christian Europe and, at the same time, a commonplace in discussions of philosophy and its divisions in the medieval schools of the twelfth and thirteenth centuries. This tradition of four liberal arts also went its way through Islam, as we can see from Kindi's treatise on the number of Aristotle's books, and from countless other pieces of evidence. The Pythagorean *quadrivium* was sometimes enlarged to include engineering and other "educational sciences," as for example in the famous *Enumeration of the Sciences* by Farabi (d. 950). Very often, though, it held its original structure without alteration, as for instance in the *Epistle on the Component Parts of the Rational Sciences* composed by Ibn Sina (d. 1037), the Avicenna of Latin tradition. But what matters for us here is that the Brethren do not list any genuine science of numbers among their propaedeutic sciences, but place the whole of mathematics in the philosophical sciences. Their list of propaedeutic sciences does include "the science of calculations and operations," but what the Brethren had in mind was no doubt a very practical and mundane use of numbers.

The other propaedeutic sciences are first and foremost sciences to do with language: reading and writing, philology and grammar, poetry and prosody. There is nothing particularly odd about their placing here. In the beginning was the Word: this seems to hold true in several Muslim classifications of the sciences, too. Thus, the first chapter of Farabi's *Enumeration of the Sciences* is devoted to the "science of the language;" and the monumental *Fihrist* of Ibn al-Nadim (d. 990), a catalogue of the sciences in its own right, similarly starts with a section which "describes the languages of the peoples, Arab and foreign, the characteristics of their methods of writing, their types of script and forms of calligraphy." That the sciences of the language should be placed at the beginning in the Epistles of the Brethren of Purity is no surprise, then. What is more striking is that they are considered from the point of view of their use in everyday life alone, for philosophers do not usually pay much attention to mundane matters. The Brethren's interest in practical matters shows again in their inclusion of the sciences of arts and crafts, buying and selling, and cultivation and breeding, which are not listed in other classifications of knowledge of the tenth and eleventh centuries. They are also surprisingly willing to recognize magic and talismans as legitimate sciences, along with alchemy and knowledge of mechanical devices. And what is one to say about the inclusion, among mundane matters, of disciplines such as *siyar* and *akhbar*, the "study of campaigns" and "history"? One would have thought that both topics had a bearing on the next world, especially *siyar*. In Islamic law books, it is a common title for the section dealing with the conduct of holy war. The word can also mean "model lives," especially in the singular, as in the *Sira* of the Prophet, whose life is a model for imitation for the believers. But maybe the whole expression simply stands for "history" in the sense of antiquities. All in all, the propaedeutic sciences here seem to have been set up primarily to serve as a kind of lumber room of mundane practices.

RELIGIOUS SCIENCES

Moving on to the second group of sciences, we note that the Brethren call it "the sciences pertaining to revealed law" (*al-'ulum al-shar'iyya*). All the sciences in this group are established for the healing of souls and the pursuit of the hereafter, as the Brethren explain, and all share the feature of being based on revealed knowledge. Whatever the role of human reason in their elaboration, all have their starting point in information originating in the divine world above us. The Brethren characterize them as "legal" (*shar'iyya*) because the core of the Revelation is a law, that is, a set of rules regulating the relationship of human beings with God and with one another. They also characterize them as "conventional" (*wad'iyya*), which may puzzle the reader, to whom "conventional" is probably a derogatory term meaning something like conforming to established usage, habit-bound, and dull. The Brethren are using the word in its earlier sense of purposefully created, established, or instituted, as opposed to inherent in nature. The subject matter of the legal sciences is divine institutions, rules which have been posited by God, and which are not open to discovery by human reason. The religion of Islam rooted in Muhammad's Revelation is here cast as a body of "conventional" or "positive" law in implicit distinction from what we would call natural law (a term the Brethren do not use) and explicit distinction from philosophy, that is, the science devoted to the truths which *are* accessible to reason, being inherent in the universe.

The Brethren identify six categories of religious sciences and mention the specialists in each of them. By the science of the Revelation (*tanzil*) they seem to mean straightforward knowledge of the Qur'anic text rather than the study of when and how it was revealed (which matters greatly for its interpretation), for the experts are identified as those who recite and memorize the book. By the science pertaining to transmissions and reports the Brethren mean the branch of learning devoted to the huge mass of statements (*Hadith*) handed down from the Prophet and his companions on which most of Islamic law is based. Islamic law in its turn is the object of the science of "jurisprudence, rules, and norms (*sunan*)." There is nothing problematic in the inclusion of any of this. What is remarkable is that there is no mention here of rationalizing theology (*kalam*), which is frequently associated with jurisprudence (*fiqh*) in Islamic classifications of the sciences. The reasons are not far to seek. Like everyone else, the Brethren seem to have turned to legal scholars for knowledge of the religious law, but for an understanding of ultimate reality they relied on the divine knowledge of their (absent) imams on the one hand and their own philosophical endeavors on the other. There was no room for theology here. "Those who know about interpretation are the imams and successors of the prophets," as they say (thus clearly identifying themselves as Shi'ites). They call interpretation *ta'wil* rather than *tafsir*, thereby implying that it was something deeper and more concerned with the inner meaning of things than the interpretations offered by others. Theology had none of the mystery or esotericism of the knowledge that the Brethren, a self-proclaimed spiritual élite, saw themselves as receiving from intermediaries between man and God. As philosophers, they were probably also contemptuous of *kalam* because it was not based on syllogistic reasoning, the only form of argument held to furnish incontestable (apodictic) proof (*burhan*). But the Brethren clearly had nothing against mysticism (*tasawwuf*), which they mention along with ascetic and devotional practices of various kinds, apparently without distinguishing between Muslim and non-Muslim forms. They also see fit to include the science of interpreting dreams, an ancient art legitimated in Islam by several prophetic reports, and also by a famous passage in the Qu'ran about Joseph in Egypt (Q. 12:43-49). Truthful dreams were held to come from God. This being so, it is often mentioned in Muslim classifications of science, as for instance in Ibn Khaldun's *Muqaddima*, where it is also ranged among the religious sciences.

PHILOSOPHICAL SCIENCES

This takes us to the third group which the Brethren call the "true (or real) sciences of philosophy" (*al-'ulum al-falsafiyya al-haqiqiyya*). It falls into four sub-groups, namely the "mathematical" (*al-riyadiyyat*), the "logical" (*al-mantiqiyyat*), the "physical" (*al-tabi'iyyat*), and the "divine" (*al-ilahiyyat*). For the present inquiry, this is also the most interesting part of the classification, since it was for the philosophical sciences that the Brethren composed their Epistles, as they themselves point out at the end of their enumeration. With this last group we come to grounds so familiar to the Brethren that they do not even bother to define it or tell their readers for what purpose these sciences exist. What we are to infer would seem to be that the philosophical sciences have not been established, but rather exist *per se*. They are not conventional (in the sense given above), but rather a natural result of the fact that humans are endowed with reason. It is perhaps in this sense that the Brethren call them "true" or "real." Though the Brethren do not explicitly say so here, there can hardly be much doubt that they regard the philosophical and the religious sciences as having the same objective, namely the happiness of the soul in the world to come. In a passage of Epistle 28, which is devoted to the limits of human knowledge, they compare the different ways of reaching salvation to different pilgrim routes converging on the Sacred House of God (*R.* III, 30-31).

THE SUBDIVISIONS OF PHILOSOPHY

Now let us proceed to the Brethren's division of philosophy itself. As is well known, Aristotle (fourth century BCE) identified physics, mathematics, and metaphysics as the three parts of what he called theoretic philosophy, whose aim was the study of the intelligible beings. Physics, he said, deals with those objects which cannot exist or be conceived of as separate from matter and motion. Mathematics, representing a higher level of abstraction, he saw as concerned with the beings which *can* be conceived of as separate from matter and motion, but which require both in order to exist. The highest level of abstraction fell to metaphysics, which dealt with those intelligible beings which are not just conceivable as separate from matter and motion, but also capable of existing without them. The Aristotelian division of speculative philosophy was transmitted to the Latin West by Boethius, who spoke in his *De Trinitate* of the three parts as *philosophia naturalis*, *mathematica,* and *theologica*. In Islam, the threefold scheme was taken up by Kindi and accepted by all his successors in the science of philosophy. The only point of discussion was the relative order of physics and mathematics. According to the so-called ontological point of view (that is, organizing things with reference to their nature), physics should come first and mathematics second, as in the scheme I have just presented. But there was also a case for placing mathematics first, given that the science of numbers formed part of the Pythagorean *quadrivium*, which was a course of propaedeutic knowledge, as we have seen.

This latter point of view seems to have prevailed in our text, for mathematics here comes before physics and metaphysics. It is followed by logic, however, and only then by physics and metaphysics, but there was a well-established tradition for this by the time of the Brethren. Following in the footsteps of the Alexandrian commentators of late antiquity, the Near Eastern philosophers who wrote in Arabic had for long been in the habit of regarding the whole set of Aristotle's logical sciences as a prerequisite "tool" – *organon* is the Greek word – for the study of every rational science. As a result, both logic and mathematics could be seen as necessary preliminaries to the general study of philosophy. In this latter case, the order in which disciplines are to be studied prevails over the ontological sequence.

The section of Epistle 7 in which the Brethren comment on the subdivisions of the philosophical group is too long to be quoted here, so I confine myself to a bare list of the elements they discuss (*R.* I, 267–274).

(1) Mathematical sciences

- arithmetic
- geometry
- astronomy
- music

(2) Logical sciences

- poetics
- rhetoric
- topics
- analytics
- sophistry

(3) Natural sciences

- the science of corporal principles

- the science of the heaven and the world
- the science of coming-to-be and passing-away
- the science of atmospheric events
- the science of minerals
- the science of plants
- the science of animals

(4) Divine sciences

- knowledge of the Creator
- the science of spiritual beings
- the science of psychic beings
- the science of governance (with five subdivisions: prophetic, royal, public, domestic, private)
- the science of the Return

This calls for a bit of explanation. One feature of this list that will immediately strike the expert is its thorough Aristotelianism. Both the general structure and the names of its parts are ultimately rooted in Aristotle's work. But there is also a glaring departure from the Aristotelian scheme in that there is no such thing here as a single science to compare with Aristotle's "science of the beings as beings" or with the *philosophia prima* of medieval scholasticism. Instead, there are five divine sciences, including the "art of governance" and the doctrine of the Return. The last three divisions of the art of governance, namely the "public," the "domestic," and the "private," fit nicely with Aristotle's subdivision of practical philosophy into politics, economics, and ethics respectively. Yet the "prophetic" and the "royal" parts stand wholly apart from any Aristotelian scheme, and should rather be understood in relation with the Brethren's highly sophisticated, and decisively Shi'ite, conception of prophetic cycles of history. As for the eschatological "science of the Return," by which the Brethren mean the return to the heavenly abode from which the human soul has fallen, it is probably best explained in the broader context of the Neoplatonic theory of emanation.

In spite of these manifold borrowings, one cannot help being impressed by the inner coherence of the Brethren's own scheme of divine sciences, for this scheme mirrors a kind of double journey between God and the ultimate goal of His creation, namely the man enabled "to know", in other words to become an accomplished philosopher. On the one hand, we notice the descending phase whereby which the human soul gradually falls down from the Creator to the individual (necessitating the "private" art of governance, i.e. ethics, at the end of the sequence). On the other hand, we find that to this descending phase corresponds an ascending phase, by which the soul of the true philosopher is able to rise up again towards its point of origin. It is no wonder, then, that the "science of the Return" gets the last place in the whole classification of sciences. The Brethren, who regularly refer to science as the food of the soul, would no doubt credit this food with the best taste, color, and smell. In passing, it is interesting to note that the Brethren speak of "knowledge" (*ma'rifa*, suggestive of recognition) rather than "science" (*'ilm*) when they come to deal with the Creator.

COMPARISON OF THE SYSTEMS

It is at this stage, I think, that we may best compare the two systems, namely the present division of philosophy and the arrangement of epistles as found in the manuscript tradition. Like the group of philosophical sciences, the whole corpus of *Rasa'il* is divided, as we have seen, into four main sections. So far, so good. But here the first discrepancies appear, for the main sections of the two systems do not exactly match one another. In spite of its title, Section I of the corpus ("mathematical sciences") includes the sciences of logic, thus appearing as a combination of the first two subdivisions of philosophy ("mathematical sciences" and "logical sciences") in Epistle 7. As a consequence of this blending, the subgroup of natural sciences is shifted to Section II of the corpus ("corporeal and natural sciences"). As for the last group mentioned in the epistle, that of divine sciences, it appears to have been split into two different sections, dealing respectively with "the sciences of the soul and of the intellect" (Section III) and "the nomic, divine and legal sciences" (Section IV). These are significant changes already. But we also notice other differences such as, for instance, the great number of epistles whose titles do not seem to match any of the subdivisions of philosophy in Epistle 7.

In the introduction of his voluminous study of the Brethren, Marquet attempted to find evidence for the view that our Epistles keep the traces of a certain vagueness, both in the order of chapters, and in the number of epistles in each section. Studying certain indications from the text itself, he arrived at the following conclusions. (1) At the time the first epistle of the group of natural sciences was written, only five epistles of Section I and seven of Section II had been compiled. (2) Some epistles from Sections I and II were later modified, whether by amplification or by division of their contents; once there was only one epistle on logic, for instance. (3) Each one of the four sections was subsequently extended or completed with the incorporation of new epistles. The comparison of our two systems confirms each one of these points. The changes, already evident for the mathematical and the physical sections, tend to become even more prominent as we come closer to the end of the corpus.

This said, the Brethren's assertion that they have devoted an epistle to each of the subdivisions remains largely valid. The encyclopaedia opens with the four sciences of the *quadrivium* (arithmetic in Epistle 1, geometry in Epistle 2, astronomy in Epistle 3, and music in Epistle 5). The only peculiarity is that an epistle on geography (Epistle 4) has been added between astronomy and music, but this is hardly surprising since geography may indeed be considered a sort of natural appendix to astronomy, which is how Ptolemy saw it in antiquity. The titles of the five epistles on logic correspond not to the five sciences mentioned in Epistle 7 (that is, poetics, rhetorics, topics, analytics, and sophistics), but rather to the famous *Book of Demonstration* – in other words, the *Posterior Analytics* (Epistle 14) – and to its four indispensable preliminaries, namely: the *Isagogue* (Epistle 10), the *Categories* (Epistle 11), the *Peri Hermeneias* or *De Interpretatione* (Epistle 12), and the *Prior Analytics* (Epistle 13). The group of natural sciences is, as we have said, the one for which the sequence has been best preserved. Each of the seven parts of physics is, indeed, the subject of an epistle (from Epistles 15 to 22), with only one noteworthy addition, namely the epistle on the quiddity of nature (Epistle 20). The most interesting point brought out by our comparison concerns the last group of sciences, where the variations can no longer be seen as negligible. Thus, apart from the science of spiritual beings, which figures as the subject of Epistle 49, the only science to which an epistle is devoted is the last one, the science of the Return – and this epistle (Epistle 38) has been placed in Section III rather than in Section IV. As for the science of governance and its subdivisions, it would be a mistake to identify it too quickly as the subject matter of Epistle 50, on the species of governance.

How are these seeming oddities be accounted for? At the risk of disappointing the reader, I would argue that these are matters which are best left unsolved for the time being. Certainly one could put forward chronological reasons and assume, for instance, that a lapse of time must have separated the writing of Epistle 7 (with its systematic and carefully reflected classification of the sciences) and the overall compilation of the *Rasa'il*. Those who, like Marquet, favor a longer chronology, could certainly claim that the authors of Epistle 7 and the final redactors of the work were not the same "Brethren of Purity." In the present state of our information, one could even surmise that the arrangement of the *Rasa'il* as we know it should not be ascribed to the authors themselves, but rather to later scribes or scholars. But all this is conjectural, and bound to remain so until we get a much clearer picture of the social, historical, and epistemological context in which our Epistles were produced, collected, and read. As for so many other vexed questions about the Brethren, this kind of speculation will have much to gain from the forthcoming edition, on a truly scientific basis, of the entire corpus of epistles.

At any rate, it is unrealistic to expect perfect correspondence between the classification of Epistle 7 and the sequence of epistles making up the actual collection, as one soon realizes if one is willing to admit that the *Rasa'il* are merely the most visible part of the Brethren's undertaking. In many places, as will be seen in Chapter 6, the Brethren refer or allude to their secret meetings known as "sessions of science" (*majalis al- 'ilm*) and make it very clear that the highest level of their teaching program has not been committed to writing. As Marquet rightly summarized it in the book mentioned above, "the Epistles are at the same time the master's book and the student's handbook, yet a handbook which must be completed with some oral teaching" (Marquet, 1973: 20). The section of our encyclopaedia for which the discrepancies with the classification of Epistle 7 are especially numerous is precisely the last one, containing the highest level of esotericism.

5

SYNCRETISM

> Know this, my Brother: we are not opposed to any science, we do not to cling fanatically to any doctrine, and we do not keep ourselves away from any of the books that the sages and the philosophers have written or composed on the various sciences and the subtle meanings which they have extracted by their intellects and observations. As for the support, assistance and foundation of our cause, they are the books of the prophets (God bless them all!), the revelation which they have set forth as well as the information, inspiration and revelation passed to them by the angels (*R.* IV, 167).

At the end of the "Case of the Animals versus Man before the King of the Jinn," one encounters a person who, judging from the many qualities he is endowed with, could easily be imagined as the Brethren's ideal man. The authors portray him as:

> a Persian in his lineage, an Arab in his religion, a true believer (*hanif*) in his doctrine, an Iraqi in his culture, a Hebrew in his experience, a follower of the Messiah in his way of proceeding, a Syrian in his piety, a Greek in his science, an Indian in his discernment, a Sufi in his way of life, angelic in his morals, heavenly in his opinion, divine in his knowledge (*R.* II, 376).

What these designations actually mean is not always self-explanatory, yet the passage as a whole stands as a good example of the Brethren's celebrated open-mindedness. The Brethren are people who will illustrate their ideas with references to Qur'anic verses, Ptolemy's *Almagest*, Hermes Trismegistus, the so-called *Theology of Aristotle*, the so-called *Golden Verses* by Pythagoras, Hadith, and Arabic and even Persian poetry (*R.* I, 137-138), and who hold themselves to be in agreement with God Most High, Abraham, Joseph, the Messiah, Muhammad, Socrates, Pythagoras, and Bilawhar (*R.* IV, 57-58). In other words, they are eclectic philosophers, and their encyclopaedia is impressive not only for the breadth of the fields it covers but also, and perhaps even more so, for the exceptionally large range of sources on which it draws.

THE GREEK HERITAGE

We got a sense of the wide variety of classical sources used by the Brethren in previous chapters, where we saw them draw on Pythagoras and Nicomachus for the *quadrivium* of mathematical sciences and their all-pervading number symbolism, on Plotinus and the Neoplatonists for their emanationist scheme of creation, on Aristotle for the overall structure of the sciences and practically every subdivision of the logical and physical sections, on Plato for the theory of proportions, and on Ptolemy for astronomy, geography, and, of course, astrology.

A more systematic survey of their sources would confirm that the great thinkers of Greek antiquity get the lion's share of attention. To the Brethren, philosophy was first and foremost philosophy in the Greek tradition. But where did they get their knowledge of the Greek philosophers from? Carmela Baffioni, who has analyzed all the passages from the *Rasa'il* which can be shown to originate in ancient Greek literature whether the Brethren were aware of this or not, shows that they were generally more familiar with the doctrines of ancient philosophers and scientists than with their actual writings, let alone their historical period or the context in which they lived. This suggests that for the most part they learnt about the philosophers' views from doxographies, that is, collections of the opinions of the Greek philosophers, rather than from their actual works, though they certainly did read Plato (perhaps usually or always in epitomes), as well as Aristotle, and Pseudo-Aristotle. The doxographies that were translated into Arabic did not contain much information about the lives and times of the philosophers, however, and though there were several histories of the philosophers in Greek, they do not seem to have been translated. The Brethren did have a fairly accurate notion of who Socrates was and how he died, but they seem to have derived their knowledge mainly from Plato's dialogues, not from historical works, for it is passages from Plato's *Phaedo* and the *Republic* that they quote. Of Plato himself they did not know much more than generalities, of Aristotle they had an even rougher picture. Like most of their contemporaries, they had never even heard of Plotinus, whose *Enneads* were familiar to them only in a paraphrase of extracts which went under the name of the "Theology of Aristotle." And they thought that Pythagoras was a sage from the city of Harran in Mesopotamia.

But who really cares? These few examples, which could be multiplied almost indefinitely, are very telling of the unembarrassed and eclectic use of sources characteristic of syncretic undertakings. As Marquet said, the Brethren's system was a "syncretism of syncretisms" (Marquet, 1973: 31), and in this respect they were worthy heirs of the Neoplatonist philosophers of late antiquity. They too were remarkably eclectic, mainly, in their case, in the use of earlier Greek schools of thought. Moreover, their founding father, Plotinus (d. 270), had worked under the influence of religious currents originating in the eastern part of the Greek-speaking world, of which he himself was a native (he was probably born in Egypt), and it was as a system adapted to this new religious climate that he revived Plato's metaphysics. The eastern slant grew more pronounced with his successors Porphyry (d. c. 301), Iamblichus (d. c. 330), and Proclus (d. c. 485). Neoplatonists also had frequent recourse to scientific theories, such as those of Ptolemy's *Almagest*, to explain aspects of Plato's assertions. All in all, their methods remind us very much of the eclectic ways of the Brethren, except that the Brethren seem to go even further than their predecessors in their attempt to harmonize the views of the ancients. Plato and his school, the Peripatetics, the Presocratics, the Stoics, and the Sceptics among the philosophers, and Ptolemy, Euclid (third century BCE), Archimedes (third century

BCE), and Galen (second century CE) among the scientists, are all made to subscribe to the same ideas.

Clearly, the Brethren worked within the Neoplatonist tradition of the Near East, and the chances are that all their information about their predecessors came via works produced by Neoplatonist philosophers. This does not solve the problem of precisely where they found what information, but it does at least account for the general features of their knowledge, for the Neoplatonists will have acted as a kind of filter in the transmission of the classical heritage, with the effect that many views were lost, while others had been blurred well before they were made available in Arabic.

Another indisputable, if less well-defined, chain of transmission is the above-mentioned city of Harran. Located in northern Mesopotamia, this city was home to a pagan population known as the Sabeans, who adhered to a curious cult based on astrological and magical practices, which they maintained even after the Muslim conquest. A significant part of the Brethren's last epistle ("The quiddity of magic, incantations and the evil eye") is devoted to a description of the Sabean initiation ritual and constitutes one of our main pieces of evidence about the Harranian cult. This first-hand statement has been examined by Marquet, according to whom Sabean paganism was a synthesis of diverse components including old Babylonian religion, Greek philosophy and religion as inherited from the Neoplatonists, Mithraism, gnosticism, and, last but not least, Hermeticism, an extremely influential current of thought from the Hellenistic period which is best defined as a syncretism of its own.

Hermeticism is especially relevant here, for it is clear that the *Corpus Hermeticum* inspired the Brethren in a very substantial way. They refer in one place to the "fourth book" of Hermes Trismegistus (namely, the *Crater* or the *Monad* of the Hermetic tradition), and it is certain that they took this "fourth book" as their model in their endeavor to define the many properties of the One. For all that, it seems that the most influential text from the *Corpus* was the introductory *Poimandres*. Its three parts – the cosmological, the anthropological, and the eschatological – contain nearly all the elements that the Brethren required to develop their theory of the soul's descent and ascent through the spheres. Not only could they find in it an overall emanation scheme and an explanation of man's double nature, they could even draw from it the meaning of the prophetic mission imparted to those who, like the seven men of the Greek text, are said to correspond to the natures of the seven planets, as we saw in Chapter 3. Even the image of the soul's falling into a slumber when it cannot turn away from the material world is present in the Hermetic treatise. The similarities between such images are admittedly much more striking than those between the actual modes of expression, so that once again one is led to conjecture that the Brethren received their knowledge through intermediaries rather than directly from the late antique work. In the case of the Hermetic corpus, the intermediaries could be the alchemist Jabir b. Hayyan (d. c. 815), the astrologer Abu Ma'shar (d. 886), or perhaps the astrological treatise to which the Brethren refer as the *Kitab al-Ustutas* and which they quote extensively in Epistle 52. In that work, which seems to be a product of the Harranian Hermeticism, the Brethren could find the all-important notion of millennial cycles connected with the successive appearance of prophets on earth. Whether the threads of these tangled skeins can always be distinguished is disputable. What is certain, however, is that it is impossible to account for the Brethren's views on astrology and magic without postulating the existence of such syncretisms before the Brethren themselves. It is hoped that further research will help us to clarify the picture, although it seems most unlikely that we shall ever succeed in reconstituting the entire network of influences, imitations, and textual borrowings.

PERSIAN AND INDIAN INFLUENCES

The Brethren may have thought of philosophy as predominantly Greek, but they certainly did not think of it as Greek alone, for Persians and Indians are also regarded as sages, and both the Persian and the Indian traditions contributed to their thought.

The Brethren worked in Iraq, a region in which at the time Persian was widely spoken and Persian culture was all-pervasive, and the profoundly Persian environment is clear, for example, in the fact that they occasionally cite Persian poetry without translating it, apparently deeming it unnecessary. More significantly, their Arabic is fluent but unsophisticated, at least in the opinion of some modern scholars, suggesting, in Alessandro Bausani's words, that it "may well have been written by someone who *thought* in another language, probably Persian" (Bausani, 1978: 11). What is certain, in any case, is that the Brethren have recourse to Persian technical terms as soon as they tackle disciplines such as astrology, zoology, and mineralogy. They also have a fair knowledge of the basic principles of Manichaeism and Zoroastrianism, and show extensive knowledge of tales about the old Sasanid kings. Finally, as has been shown in detail in Chapter 3, the Brethren make full use of an astrological theory which is undoubtedly of Iranian origin, although they may well have found it in the writings of Abu Ma'shar. I refer here to the Saturn–Jupiter conjunctions and to their transfers through the triplicities of the zodiac, an extremely successful theory that was used to account for a multitude of changes on the surface of the earth.

The Indian contribution is also significant, if not perhaps not as all-pervading as the Iranian. Thus the Brethren tell several "Animal Stories" and "King Stories" borrowed from India, most of them probably via Persian translations or adaptations. All are of an essentially edifying character, as Netton stresses. The outstanding example of the "Animal" genre in Islamic literature is *Kalila wa-Dimna* (originally known as the "Fables of Bidpai"), on which the Brethren modeled their own "Case of the Animals versus Man" in Epistle 22. Other allusions to that work are scattered throughout the *Rasa'il*, and we have already referred in Chapter 1 to the story of the ring-dove which may be the source of the very name of the Ikhwan al-Safa'. Among the "King Stories," the Brethren seem to have had a predilection for the equally moralizing "Legend of Budhasaf [sometimes spelled Yudasaf or, as in the *Rasa'il*, Budasaf] and Bilawhar." This set of popular writings, which has its ultimate origins in the biography of the Buddha, came to be widely-known in Pahlavi and then in Arabic literature. In the Arabic adaptations, Budhasaf is portrayed as a powerful but insensitive prince who only understands in very old age the misery of his own situation and has to seek advice about it. Bilawhar is a hermit from Ceylon who persuades him to abandon his position and live the life of an ascetic. It is clear why the Brethren were fond of such stories, of which some pleasing examples are given in their epistles, particularly in Epistle 48 ("The modalities of the call to God"). One of them is the story of the prince who, drunk after his own marriage ceremony, sleeps with a corpse in the belief that it is his bride and only realizes the day after how wrong he has been. The metaphor of the soul unable to escape from its corporeal prison or, more exactly, tomb, is quite transparent, and would probably have been appreciated by Plato himself. What Netton does not mention is that India made an appreciable contribution to the Brethren's cosmology. As has been already shown, the Brethren attached great importance to a number of enormously long astronomical periods ultimately derived from a work by the Indian astronomer Brahmagupta in 628 CE. Among others, they mention as coming from a certain *Zij al-Sindhind* a 360,000-year cycle, which they define as the period required for all the planets to come back into conjunction in the first degree of Aries. Here their immediate source is likely to be one of the many books on conjunctions compiled by Abu Ma'shar, who for his part called this period the "Cycle of the Persians." In Epistle 16 ("The Heavens and the world"), the Brethren tell two stories designed to illustrate the conjunctional Great Year. The first has a properly Islamic resonance about it, since it compares the movements of the planets to the pilgrims' circumambulations of the Sacred Ka'ba. But the second is presented as a mathematical problem formulated by the "wise men of India" (*R.* II, 40): the reader is invited to compute how much time it will take for seven individuals with seven different speeds to complete tours around a circular city.

RECONCILING PROFANE AND SACRED WISDOM

These are the main influences behind the Brethren in their grand effort to understand the realities of the world as rationally apprehended and transmitted over the centuries by humankind. Between them, these heritages cover the whole range of those "philosophical and real sciences" about which the authors claim to have written their set of epistles. And yet the Brethren, as many of their contemporaries in Islam, had to face another, perhaps even more daunting, task of reconciling all this with the "religious and conventional sciences" that they mention in their classification of the sciences in Epistle 7. From the first to the last epistle we can see in almost every paragraph a conspicuous attempt at harmonizing the human and the divine sciences. Epistemologically, the reconciliation of reason and faith is justified on the grounds that both are said to be of divine origin and pursue the same objective, which is the purification of the soul. At the end of Epistle 28, which is dedicated to the limits of human knowledge, the Brethren explain:

> Now you must know that the sciences based on human wisdom and those based on prophetic revelation are fields of study which agree about the aim they pursue – the fundamental point – while disagreeing about the ramifications. For it is said that the ultimate aim of philosophy is imitation of the divinity to the best of man's ability, as we have shown in all our epistles. It rests on four properties: first, knowledge of the realities of existing things; secondly, profession of faith in valid opinions; thirdly, the achievement of a high morality and a praiseworthy temper; and fourthly, pure deeds and good acts. The aim of these properties in their turn is the refinement of the soul and its elevation from a state of deficiency to one of accomplishment, passing from the limits of potentiality to manifestation in reality, so that the soul may secure its survival and permanence and eternal life in a blessed state together with others of the same kind in the company of angels. Similarly, the aim of prophethood and the law is to refine the human soul and to reform it, so as to rescue it from the Hell of the world of coming-to-be and passing-away, and enable it to reach the Paradise and the blessed state of its denizens in the spacious world of the spheres and the amplitude of the heavens, breathing the wind and the smells mentioned in the Qur'an (*R*. III, 30).

This presentation was likely to convince only the converted, but then converted is precisely what the authors of the *Rasa'il* could expect their readers to be. It is a good example of the Brethren's tendency to throw in an allusion to the Qur'an in a manner suggesting complete agreement between it and their system, without trying to prove it in detail, presumably because it would be an uphill task.

THE INTERPRETATION OF THE QUR'AN

Qur'anic quotations are extremely numerous in the Epistles. As Netton nicely put it: "The corpus of the *Rasa'il* is saturated with the Qur'an like a sponge and innumerable quotations bear witness to the Ikhwan's deep familiarity with the basic scriptural text of orthodox Islam. In it the Ikhwan are able to find the source, or at least the justification, for many of their ideas" (Netton, 2002: 79). Indeed, they seem to find things in it that may be less than obvious to the reader, for sometimes they operate with very broad similarities, such as that between the Garden, that is, Paradise, in the Qur'an and what is commonly referred to in Hadith as "the (paradisical) Basin," or even between Paradise and the divine atmosphere mentioned in the Pythagorean *Golden Verses*. At other times, one simply cannot see exactly how a Qur'anic quotation is meant to illustrate a particular point. This is true particularly when one reaches the end of an epistle, with its customary series of admonitions and exhortations, where they will throw in quotations or references to the scripture in much the same loose way as in the quotation above. Are we then to take it that the Brethren are using the Qur'an as a mere "cloak" or a "smoke-screen for doctrines which were entirely un-Qur'anic?" This is what Netton assumes. But it would imply that the Brethren were insincere, which does not ring true to me. Still, it remains a fact that their use of the Qur'an exhibits two further peculiarities which are worth considering.

First and most obviously, their references to the Qur'an are highly selective. Just as they are happy to allude to the Qur'an in the loosest of ways to suggest agreement, so they only pick out Qur'anic statements that could be understood as accounts of, or expressions of agreement with, their own doctrines. They display much interest in the great biblical figures whose missions preceded and heralded that of Muhammad, and they have a particular fondness for the Qur'anic stories of the warning prophets sent to remind their people against the danger of forgetting God's message. It cannot be said that the preaching of these prophets has much in common with the Brethren's ideas, but no religious thinker struggling to get his message past a hostile religious establishment could fail to identify with these figures, who are depicted in the Qur'an as invariably mocked or threatened with expulsion until God punishes the thankless unbelievers. We need not accuse the Brethren of using the Qur'an as a smokescreen or cloak when they refer to these warning prophets. Of course they were trying to secure authority for what outsiders would regard as un-Qur'anic views, but in this they were merely behaving like normal readers of the book: all would find their own views in it, and the distance between what people found and what the Qur'an actually says, in the opinion of modern scholars, was often every bit as great in the case of impeccably Sunni authors as in that of the Ikhwan. The Qur'an speaks time and again of warning prophets, giving the Brethren a rich gallery of figures to identify with, from Moses struggling against Pharaoh to Hud trying to persuade 'Ad, his people, to listen to him: different prophets, different peoples, different epochs, but only one lesson to be taught. Given that the circumstances under which a prophet was sent were always adverse, the Brethren inferred that he would have to cure human souls in the same way as the physician healed human bodies.

Second, the Brethren interpret the Qur'an allegorically. This is as might be expected, given that they were Shi'ites, and indeed given that they were philosophers too, for it long had been, and would remain, a commonplace in philosophical circles that the statements of the Revelation were symbols and parables for higher truths. The Revelation was full of secrets, as some put it. The philosophers typically complemented the symbolic truths of the Revelation, meant for the masses, with the naked truths of reason, meant for the philosophers, but the Brethren credited their allegorical interpretation (*ta'wil*) of the Qur'an to their imams, as has been mentioned earlier. Against the literal meaning of the Revelation, accessible to all, they thus postulated a higher meaning derived from another kind of revelation, accessible only to a few. This allowed them to use the Qur'an with great latitude. In their Epistle 40 ("Causes and effects"), for example, they mention some of the hypotheses advanced in interpretation of the mysterious letters which appear at the beginning of many suras (or chapters) of the Qur'an. The "orthodox" stance is that the letters are a divine mystery and that it is vain trying to penetrate it. The Brethren mention this position, but they also offer interpretations such as that each letter corresponds to a numerical value or that it is an abbreviation of a word. They plainly do not think that these letters are a mystery to those few who are qualified to understand them, evidently counting themselves among those chosen few. Many other examples could be found of the Brethren's rather free approach to the Holy Book and their readiness to overstep the limits of a purely literal reading of God's word.

THE LEVELING OF SACRED AUTHORITIES

Given that these peculiarities do not imply insincerity, we need not doubt that the Brethren regarded the revealed book of Islam as incomparably superior to, and therefore more authoritative than, any piece of literature produced by ordinary humans. In fact, they even identify it as superior to any other revealed book in Epistle 31 ("The reasons of the difference in languages, graphic figures and expressions"), in the following statement:

> Islam will prevail over all other religions, and Arabic over all other languages, and religion will be one, as God Most-High has said: "It is He who has sent His messenger with guidance and the religion of truth, that He may make it prevail over all religion, though the unbelievers may dislike it" (Q. 9:33; 61:9). The reason why the religion of the Prophet will prevail over all other religions, and his language over all other languages, is that the Qur'an is the most honoured "recitation" (*Qur'an*) that God Most-High has revealed, and the noblest book that He has affirmed, and that for all the variety of their languages, none of the nations can translate it from the Arabic language it is in to any other language. For it is absolutely impossible

> to translate it into another language, owing to its concision and brevity (*R.* III, 164-165).

But it is hard to set any store by this statement, which mouths conventional orthodoxy in what one would assume to be a precautionary vein. Elsewhere, the Brethren's natural inclination is rather to put the Qur'an on a par with the other holy books, all regarded as authoritative. Netton notes that "the Ikhwan frequently cite the Gospel, usually with the Torah and Qur'an but occasionally with 'the prophetical books' or the Psalms, as an example of a prophetic, revealed book, thereby underlining the particular respect which Islam always showed towards 'the People of the Book'"(Netton, 2002: 54). In fact, the Epistles abound in quotations taken indiscriminately from any of the books which the Brethren would consider to be of divine provenance, especially the canonical and extra-canonical heritage from the Christians and the Jews. In Epistle 52, for example, they seek to validate the use of magic with reference to Qur'anic verses about licit magic as well as an account about the enchanted hunting coat of Adam which they claim to take from the Torah, though it actually comes from the Midrash. They introduce their account as follows:

> Now let us go back to what has been said about it [that is, magic] by the other lawgiver prophets and what one finds in the books they believe in and profess to be authentic. Among these things there is what is written in the Torah and taken into account and recognized as authentic by two of the communities alike, namely the Jews and the Christians. For the Torah is found in the hands of the Jews and the Christians, in Hebrew, Syriac and Arabic, and there is no disagreement among them about it. On the contrary, they agree on its authenticity and the truth of its contents (*R.* IV, 291).

Here the Ikhwan seem to treat the Torah and the Gospels as equally authoritative. It does not follow that they considered them as just as authoritative as the Qur'an itself, of course, but it will probably come as a surprise to most readers that nowhere in the Epistles are these other scriptures said to be less reliable than the holy book of Islam, and the passage discussed in the next section strongly suggests that they regarded all revealed books as equally authoritative.

THE ULTIMATE BOOKS

The Brethren reveal their attitude to the relationship between philosophical and revealed books in an interesting passage, first found in Epistle 45 and repeated almost verbatim in Epistle 48, in which they identify the categories of information in which they believe the truth to be accessible. Each category is called a book, and the passage neatly encapsulates the Brethren's epistemology or science of knowledge:

> Our sciences are drawn from four (kinds of) books: first, the books composed by wise men and philosophers on mathematics and natural sciences; secondly, the revealed books brought by the prophets – upon them the grace of God – such as the Torah, the Gospel, the Qur'an (*al-furqan*, literally "the Proof"), and other prophetic books whose meanings come from revelation, including the secrets hidden in them. Thirdly, the books of nature, that is, the forms of existing things as they are now: the structure of the spheres, the divisions of the zodiac, the movements of the stars and the measures of their bodies, the vicissitudes of time, the transmutation of the elements, the categories of what is produced in terms of minerals, animals and plants, and the varieties of what is manufactured by man. All these are forms and allusions which hint at subtle meanings and delicate secrets. People see what is apparent in them, yet they do not know the inner meanings of the subtleties of the Creator's attribute (praise be upon Him!). Fourthly, the divine books, which no one touches but the pure angels, and which are in the hands of noble and pious scribes. These are the substances of the souls and their genera, species, and particulars, the variations that they (the souls) create in the bodies, the movements they effect in them, their government of them, and their sitting in judgement of them (*R.* IV, 42-43).

Of the four categories of books mentioned, only the first two are books in the literal sense of the word, that is, the works composed by wise men and philosophers on mathematics and natural sciences on the one hand, and the books revealed to prophets on the other. The third and the fourth are quite different in character and belong rather to what I would call a "virtual library." The third is "the books of nature," a concept familiar to the Western tradition too, though there the expression tends to be the "book of nature" in the singular. It means much the same in both cases, that is to say, the regularities or laws of nature. The idea is that by understanding these regularities, one comes to understand the Creator behind them. Nature is seen as an attribute of God, or an emanation of His characteristics, and whoever understands its laws gets to know "the mind of God." But the fourth and last category is wholly unfamiliar to a Western reader. The divine books "which no one touches but the pure angels" are something like the ultimate key to the human condition. They take the form of plans or blueprints for human souls. Each soul descends into a human body equipped with a program from this book, so to speak, a metaphysical equivalent of a genetic code, and each spends its life in the body acting out this program.

The four "books" are arranged hierarchically according to the degree of esoteric knowledge they contain, for it is only in such knowledge that a true understanding of the cosmos and the human condition will be found. The books by the sages and philosophers (two words meaning much the same) form the lowest level, as the only products of the human mind to be included. All writings by non-philosophers, whether legal, theological, or other, are tacitly dismissed as worthless for the enterprise. At the next level we find the books revealed to the prophets. The Brethren clearly do think that the Qur'an ranked above philosophical writings (as argued above), they just did not think that it did so alone: all revealed books here occupy the same level in the hierarchy of knowledge, all are superior to literature produced by ordinary humans, and all seem to be endowed with the same authority. All in their turn rank below the secrets of nature, the regularities behind the workings of the cosmos, or what we would call natural laws. The understanding hidden in these laws is open only to a few, though all human beings observe their workings every day. Finally, the heavenly books are wholly inaccessible to human beings, at least as long as they are imprisoned in bodies. Only purified angels touch these books, as they say.

Elsewhere, as we have seen in Chapter 2, the Brethren make it clear that human beings may hope to rise to the level of such angels themselves one day, but only when they purify their souls here on earth to the point where they can shed the body for good when they die. In the meantime, how are humans to get access to the heavenly book, the ultimate key to the human condition? They do not tell us, but one assumes that they would say that they relied on their imams – or in other words on their own imaginative intelligence, for though the imams had once been real human beings, they were now constructs of the Brethren's minds. Envisaging their own esoteric speculation as knowledge taught by such constructs did however make it easier for them to talk about their own ideas and, above all, it endowed them with an authority that they would otherwise lack.

6

IDEALISM

> If you, my pious and merciful brother and your brethren, feel eager to read those books in order to learn what they contain and to understand their meanings and know their secrets, then come and attend a session of your virtuous brethren and noble friends so that you may listen to what they say and see their innate qualities and get to know their way of life. Perhaps you will be molded by their characters and refined by their good manners, and your soul will wake up from the sleep of negligence and torpor of ignorance (*R.* IV, 168).

The present chapter will focus on the way the Brethren appear to have situated themselves *vis-à-vis* their contemporaries and conceived of their mission in this world. It will examine features which can be identified as typically Shi'ite, some of them even as typically Ismaili, but the purpose is not to determine their sectarian affiliation, merely to convey a general sense of their orientation.

OTHER CONFESSIONS

The text cited at the beginning of the previous chapter shows how the Brethren saw themselves as receptive to wisdom from wherever it came: they did not cling fanatically to any sort of doctrine or reject books by any of the philosophers, as they say. This passage has often been singled out to illustrate their open-mindedness, and one could add many others of the same kind. This is not, of course, to say that the Brethren professed a kind of general and indiscriminate ecumenism, let alone that they refrained from criticism of people whom they perceived as enemies of wisdom. But they did show appreciation for people whose aims they recognized even when they belonged to confessional communities or sects other than their own.

Thus they seem to be quite favorable to Christianity. The figure of Jesus appealed to them as a model of piety, compassion, courage, and humility, and several passages show that the Brethren also admired the reclusive and ascetic life of Christian monks. In Epistle 50 ("The species of governance") they even recommend celibacy as an ideal for members of the brotherhood, an attitude which is not commonly found in Islam, though it is certainly not unknown: Sufis often debated the pros and cons of marriage for people devoted to a spiritual life. The Brethren repeatedly invite their audience to read the Gospel, too. These are among the considerations which prompted Stanley Lane-Poole to conclude that "In their ideal of the higher life, indeed, the Brotherhood of Purity belong to Christianity rather than to Islam" (Lane-Poole, 1960: 207). Few today will share Poole's assumption that anything shared with Christianity must "belong to" Christianity, as if ideas which pass from one circle to another remain the property of the former and as if there could not be a spectrum of attitudes or a variety of sub-cultures within Islam; but he is certainly right that the Brethren had strong affinities with Christianity, suggesting that it was from a Christian environment that their forebears stemmed.

Jews were not considered with the same degree of empathy or understanding, possibly because the Qur'an itself is harsher on them than on Christians and possibly also because the Brethren brought antipathy to Judaism with them from their Christian background. In any case, there is no sign in the Epistles that they knew much about them. They do not often mention Jews, and when they do, it is usually as representatives of the legalistic approach to religion of which they disapproved. Thus the anecdotes and popular narratives in Epistle 9 include an adaptation of what appears to be the story of the Jew and the Good Samaritan, here a Jew and a Zoroastrian, in which the former tries to justify his lack of compassion for humans who did not belong to his own confessional community on the grounds that his religion was responsible for his education (*R.* I, 308–310); the suggestion seems to be that lack of compassion was an intrinsic feature of Judaism. The characterization is crude, but one probably should not attach too much weight to it as evidence for the Brethren's view of Jews, given that the story is a parable. They often seem to use "Jew" as a term for representatives of any kind of legalistic religion, traditionalist Muslims included.

The Brethren did not have much to say about Zoroastrianism, or Buddhism, but they often refer to the fact that they lived in a world dominated by a large number of competing religions, sects, and schools, and they did their best to make sense of this by comparing the many belief systems to the many pilgrim routes leading to a single sanctuary (*R.* II, 367). In principle, it would seem, the highest truth was accessible from within all these communities, not just Islam. But the precise relationship between confessional communities and the highest truth in their work is a subject in need of further investigation.

Moving on to their attitude to other Muslims, we may note that though they were not mystics themselves, they counted mysticism – or Sufism (*tasawwuf*), as the Muslims called it – as one of the "religious and conventional sciences" and associated it with "remembrance, exhortations and asceticism" (*R.* I, 267); they were even willing to apply the term "Sufi" to themselves: in the opening lines of the encyclopaedia they say that the 52 epistles were compiled from the words of "the sincere friends, the Sufis" (*R.* I, 21). So it is certainly not by chance that the Epistles contain a wide variety of words or expressions familiar from the vocabulary of Sufism as it had begun to develop in the ninth and tenth centuries. The very appellation "Ikhwan al-Safa'," with which the Brethren characterize themselves by sincere fraternal relations, could be a Sufi expression. There are many suggestive parallels to be drawn between Sufi literature (and indeed mystical literature in general) and the *Rasa'il*. Epistle 46 ("The quiddity of Faith") looks especially promising in this respect, for here one finds a carefully compiled and detailed list of the six conditions of true faith, which sounds a decisively mystic tone. The sequence is:

trust (*tawakkul*), sincere devotion (*ikhlas*), patience (*sabr*), contentment (*rida'*), fear (*khawf*), and asceticism (*zuhd*). The same epistle also contains a long edifying fable about a repentant hedonist and an ascetic (*R.* IV, 90-98).

RELIGIOUS LAW

As the Brethren admired spiritually inclined Christians and Sufis, so they disliked legally orientated Jews and Muslims. They obviously had their reservations about religious law as an avenue to salvation, whether in an Islamic or other context. Religious law (*shari'a al-din*) was coercive, as they said at the end of their final epistle (on magic), since it was something conventional (*wad'i*) and traditional (*sunni*) which pertained to this world (*dunyawi*) (*R.* IV, 460); by contrast, religion as such (*din*) was something freely chosen by believers in their heart of hearts. The Brethren had no doubt that the religious law was necessary at the level of society and the individual alike: it made for discipline and order in this world, and also served as a precondition for one's spiritual purification; it was a remedy for sick souls, as they liked to put it (e. g. *R.* II, 11). They just did not think that the cure it offered sufficed to save anyone from this corrupt world (and salvation from this world through the acquisition of angelic status was what they were striving for). That the law has limited value is implicit throughout the epistles, but there are also passages in which the Brethren discuss it with a certain degree of explicitness.

For example, the Brethren often allude to the fact that since the religious law is a matter of external behavior rather than of inner conviction, it easily becomes a refuge for opportunists, who will disguise the wickedness of their souls through all kinds of hypocritical claims and practices. By way of example they usually refer to the unbelievers of the Prophet's time who embraced Islam without conviction and whom the Qur'an itself names Hypocrites (*munafiqun*), but no doubt it was contemporaries they had in mind.

The fact that hypocrites would abuse the law does not of course mean that there was anything wrong with the law itself. But the Brethren explicitly characterize the law, or more precisely the letter of the revelation in general, as the lowest form of religion in Epistle 42 ("Views and religions"). Here they say that there are three categories of believers (*R.* III, 511-512). The lowest category is occupied by the "common mass" (*'amma*) of "women, children and (other) ignorant people," presumably meaning all those who were not schooled in the religious sciences. Only exoteric (*zahir*) religious knowledge was suitable to them, they say, with reference to knowledge of the prayers, fasting, alms, and other aspects of ritual worship, accounts of the past, traditions (from the Prophet and other early figures), edifying stories, and the like. In short, people of the first category could not rise above the plain, literal, and practical meaning of religious institutions. In the second category were the "intermediate people" (*mutawassitin*), whom the Brethren do not otherwise define, but whom they deem capable of studying jurisprudence (*fiqh*), just conduct, and the meaning of words, on the basis of research into exegesis (*tafsir*), revelation (*tanzil*), allegorical interpretation (*ta'wil*), and the plain (*muhkamat*) and obscure (*mutashabihat*) verses of the Qur'an (as they say in a rather odd list); it was appropriate for people in this category to seek arguments and proofs for everything and not to take religion on trust when independent judgment (*ijtihad*) and theoretical enquiry (*nazar*) is possible. Apparently, the Brethren here have in mind jurists and theologians, or in other words scholars who applied reason to the letter of the revelation, but who did not go so far as to study philosophy, the highest form of religion in the Brethren's view. Sunni or Shi'i, such scholars ranked higher than the common people because of their ability to probe the deeper meaning of the revelation by means of reason, but they still fell short of the third and highest level.

The believers in the third category are the "chosen few" (*khawass*) who have become strong in both the religious *and* the rational sciences, so that they are in a position to study the hidden secrets of religion, which can only be touched by those purified of filthy desire, arrogance, and hypocrisy. The secrets of religion, the Brethren inform us, are the meanings which the lawgivers have received from the angels and passed down in their revealed books, hiding them behind subtle allusions (*isharat*) and symbols (*rumuz*). Among such books, they mention the Torah, the Gospel, the Psalms, the Furqan (i.e. the Qur'an), and the scrolls of the Prophets, continuing with a long list of symbols and allusions of the type they have in mind: God's pact with Adam, Iblis's disobedience, the tree of eternity, the balance of judgment, the *barzakh*, and so on. They do not, of course, disclose what these elements are symbolic of, since that would mean that it was knowledge accessible to all. Instead, they conclude by urging the reader to make every effort to join the people of the highest rank.

What are the relative prospects of the three categories of believers as far as salvation is concerned? The Brethren do not explicitly tell us, but if the law sufficed for salvation, all three categories of believers would be saved, and where then would be the reward for the use of reason? The answer that the pleasure of understanding is a reward in itself would not have commended itself to them. Either the Brethren envisaged salvation as graded, with different types and degrees of felicity for each of the three categories (along lines suggested by Farabi in some of his works), or else they held that only the members of the third category were saved, since it was only people in this category who were deemed worthy of studying the secrets received from the angels. Since the Brethren held that salvation lay in rising to the rank of angels, there can be little doubt that it was to the second view that they subscribed. This is not of course to say that they dismissed traditional piety, simple virtues, or religious scholarship as without merit, let alone that they condemned the vast majority of Muslims to eternal hellfire (a concept they do not seem to have accepted in a literal sense). Rather, they seem to have believed that those who were not saved would be reborn at different levels reflecting the moral status they had achieved in their earlier life, so that they too would be able eventually to rise to angelic rank, as we have seen in the discussion of the Brethren's view on eschatology in Chapter 2. Even domestic animals would be rewarded for their faithful and all too often painful service, it would seem, by being reborn as humans and thus able to start the upward climb.

Neither angels nor animals needed the law, the former because they were perfect, the latter because they had no moral responsibility (except in the Animals versus Humans fable, in which they appear as protagonists of natural religion). But moral responsibility was the essence of the human condition, and without the law one could not start the climb towards perfection. But without philosophy one could not get to the top.

Would the law form part of the human condition forever? The Brethren did not think so. In this current cycle, all humans needed the law and other aspects of positive religion because they were sick, having disobeyed God and been expelled from Paradise (*R.* II, 320-321). The prophets were physicians of the souls, as the animals say in the Animals versus Humans fable (*R.* II, 325), using a popular metaphor of great antiquity in the Near East which the Brethren invoke elsewhere as well. It was for this reason that the natural religion of the animals had been replaced with all the burdensome institutions of conventional religion characteristic of human civilization. But in common with most Ismailis, the Brethren held, or at least hoped, that the law with which the prophets did their healing would be unnecessary in the next cycle.

The key question was whether one had to wait for the new cycle to dispense with conventional religion or whether a few select souls could reach perfection in the here and now. Needless to say, the Brethren do not openly answer this question in the affirmative. It is, none the less, hard to avoid the impression that they held this to be possible, and Maqdisi, supposedly one of the authors of the Epistles, is credited with an explicit endorsement of this view in Tawhidi's "Book of Pleasure and Conviviality" (an important source which we met in the discussion of the date and authorship of our Epistles). Maqdisi here says that the religious law is medicine for the sick while philosophy is medicine for the healthy, in the sense that it enables people to preserve their health and to achieve eternal life; the law fosters virtues (in sick souls) by making them accept things on authority, philosophy teaches virtues (to healthy people) by means of demonstrative proofs; both law and philosophy are necessary, the former for the common people (*al-'amma*), the latter for the select few (*al-khassa*) (*Imta'*, ii, 11). What Maqdisi is expounding here is the same idea as that underlying the account of the three categories of believers, though there are only two categories in his account. Both statements cast conventional religion as a set of basically coercive institutions that prevent people from behaving in the utterly selfish and immoral manner that would have been characteristic of them if God had left them alone without giving them a law. For the common mass of mankind that is all that religion can ever be. Those who have overcome their vicious tendencies by internalization of the law, however, can dispense with the external acts of worship to concentrate on higher things: in both accounts the law is cast as a medicine that you stop taking when you are cured, or as a crutch that you throw away when you have learnt to walk. It is an idea attested for Batinis, that is "esotericists," elsewhere as well.

THE TRUE IMAM

In their discussions of conventional religion the Brethren sound much like other philosophers of a Neoplatonist bent, but they were also Shi'ites. Where on the Shi'ite map did they locate themselves?

There is an interesting answer to this question at the beginning of the already oft-quoted Epistle 48 ("The call to go to God"). This epistle is written in a manner suggesting that one is intended to identify its author as the hidden imam, who here reviews a variety of groups whom he identifies as "our brethren and members of our party" (*min ikhwanina wa-ahli shi'atina*), though it soon becomes clear that only a small number of them are members of the Brethren's spiritual brotherhood. The rest belong to "our party" only in the sense that they are members of "'Ali's party" (*shi'at 'Ali*). In other words, in this passage the Brethren cast their imam as the leader of all Shi'ites, not of a particular group of them, though they acknowledge that they do not all in fact recognize him: all *ought* to accept his authority (and thus that of his representatives, the Brethren themselves). Having identified their imam as the true director of 'Ali's party in its entirety, they proceed to divide this party into three main groups.

The first consists of those "who are learned in the field of religion, know the secrets of prophecies and are well-trained in philosophical disciplines" (*R.* IV, 145). It is to these accomplished brethren, as we have seen in Chapter 3, that the imminence of the conjunction is to be revealed. The reference here is clearly to the Brethren themselves, "our party" in the sense of their own tiny spiritual brotherhood.

The second group consists of brethren of whom "some are in doubt about our [i.e. the imam's] existence and perplexed with regard to the question whether we are alive," while "others are convinced of the fact that we are alive, yet neglectful of our cause and ignorant of our secrets." The reference here is to Shi'ites who sat on the fence. Some were not sure that the imam in question was actually alive, others were convinced of it but still failed to support the cause as they should, though "all of them expect the manifestation of our cause and are eager for our days to come and desirous to support our cause" (*R.* IV, 146). The Brethren would like to convert these doubting or uncommitted Shi'ites, as they make clear by inviting their reader to provide these people with such epistles "as their souls desire."

The third group consists of "those from our confession who admit our excellence and also the excellence of the people of our house, but who ignore our sciences and pay no attention to our secrets and wisdom; among other things, they deny our existence, refuse to believe that we are still alive, and on top of that they revile our followers who affirm our existence and expect the manifestation of our cause; they oppose with these latter and gang up against them, detesting" (*R.* IV, 147). Here we have Shi'ites who accept the virtue of all members of the holy family but who do not follow the Brethren's imam, whom they regard as dead and whose followers in the present they detest.

The entire passage makes excellent sense if we take the Brethren to have been Ismailis. Their imam would in that case be a descendant of Ismail (d. 765), the son of Ja'far al-Sadiq (d. 765) who in the Ismaili view had inherited Ja'far's position. Most Shi'ites had rejected him, giving their allegiance to other sons of Ja'far, such as 'Abd Allah al-Aftah or Musa al-Kazim, or to none at all (see chart, p. xvii). When the Brethren claim to have a hidden imam whom their opponents regard as dead, the reference is presumably to Ismail's son Muhammad, the mahdi of most Ismailis until c. 890 and of practically all the eastern Ismailis thereafter. When they tell us that others declare him dead and hate his followers, we take them to be referring to the Imamis. Their hidden imam was a descendant of Musa al-Kazim (d. 799); he had gone into hiding in 874, and all communication with him was deemed to have been cut off in 941, starting the so-called "greater occulation" which would continue until the end of time, when the descendant in question would reappear as the mahdi. The big difference between the two positions lay not so much in the choice between the two imams as in that between two (or, in practice, several) religious organizations with sharply divergent religious and political aims; and what we learn here is that some people were undecided, finding it difficult to make up their minds on the question whether one or the other imam was alive. There were also sympathizers who would not properly commit themselves to the cause, we learn. All this is as might be expected. The main interest of the passage lies in the unambiguous manner in which the Brethren claim to be the true leaders of the entire body of Shi'ites, or at least all those who traced a continuous imamate from the time of the Prophet until the present (*ashab nasaq al-imama*, as they were technically known).

Having effectively declared their hands as Ismailis, the Brethren continue by having the imam lash out against people who used Shi'ism (*tashayyu'*) as a veil (*sitran*) for all sorts of horrendous misdeeds (*R.* IV, 147). "They commit every forbidden act, leave off what they have been commanded, and if they are forbidden something, they do it," he says, perhaps with reference to the antinomian behavior of the Ismailis in Bahrayn in the 930s. Worse still, he continues, some of these people "are affiliated to us in body, though not in soul" and call themselves Alids (*'alawiyya*), but they are just lowly people who know nothing about the imams except their physical relationship and who have no religious learning, no jurisprudence, no prayer, no alms, no sanctuary, or no jihad, who respect nothing, hold back from nothing, and who commit every forbidden deed. The reference could be to the Fatimids, depicted in lurid colors and condemned as antinomians like those in Bahrayn. These people were the worst enemies of the Shi'ites and the furthest removed from the truth except for the Hashimites who thought that their exalted genealogies would save them, presumably meaning the many noble Alids who kept genealogies, frequented the court, and served in official functions at this time, such as the family of al-Sharif al-Radi and al-Murtada.

Having denounced the men in power, the Brethren move on to the popular manifestations of Shi'ism, which were no more to their taste. Some people use Shi'ism as a source of income (*maksiban*), they have the imam say, giving as their examples people "such as (hired) female mourners and story-tellers, for whom Shi'ism consists of nothing but 'disavowal, vilification, calumniation, and cursing'" – a reference to the habit, shared by most Shi'ites, of vilifying the first three caliphs as usurpers of 'Ali's rights and cursing the Umayyad caliph and his generals who had killed Husayn at Karbala'. Equally bad is "weeping with the female mourners and loving those who profess Shi'ism while abandoning the pursuit of science and the study of the Qur'an and the religion." Such people make it their hallmark to "stay at the shrines of martyrs and visit tombs, like women who have lost their children; they weep when we (imams) lose our bodies, but it is for their own souls that they should weep first!"

Finally, the Brethren denounce those "who claim that imams hear prayers and answer supplications": such people do not know the truth of their own beliefs, they say. Others, they say, "believe that the expected imam (*al-imam al-muntazar*) hides himself out of fear of the opponents." "Not at all," they write, clearly with reference to the man whom they regard as the true imam; "he is well in sight (*zahir*) among them and he knows them, but they deny him." That the imam was hiding out of fear of his opponents was a well-known Imami tenet. Since the Brethren's imam was also absent, it is at first sight difficult to see how they could claim that there was anything different about him, but they denounce the Imami belief elsewhere as well: he who thinks that the expected imam is in hiding, not daring to appear for fear of his enemies, will spend his life impatiently waiting for this imam, only to die in misery without knowing who he is (*R.* III, 523).

To politically active Ismailis, the difference between the hidden imam of the Imamis and their own mahdi lay in the fact that the latter's coming was so imminent that one could take political action on his behalf, above all by starting to fight his enemies, whereas the return of his Imami counterpart was as indeterminate as the second coming of Jesus. But this does not seem to be what matters to the Brethren. Rather, they are dismissing the idea of an imam hiding because of enemies: it is as bad an idea as the suggestion that Jesus was killed by enemies, they say, explaining that it left the believers plagued by feelings of pity and hopes of revenge (*R.* III, 523). There was no point in awaiting the coming of the imam, for he was already present and knew his adherents. In fact, the Imamis would hardly have disagreed with that, but they did not know the truth of their own beliefs, as the Brethren insist. One did not approach the imams with all this weeping over martyrs, cursing of caliphs, touching of shrines, and praying for this and that. Rather, one reached them by assimilating their virtues, and this in turn one achieved by study, above all by study of philosophy, not by crude emotionalism.

All this does something to confirm the common idea that the Brethren were Ismailis of an unaffiliated type. They did not belong to any sect, and they were too eirenic, and also too élitist and esoteric, to found one themselves. Most Ismailis, indeed most Shi'ites, came across to them as misguided, as should be clear from the above. Elsewhere, they deride the views of those whom they call the "Seveners" (*musabbi'a*) because they seem to be obsessed with the number seven (*R.* III, 180), which must be a reference to Ismailis of some kind, given the latter's predilection for the number seven. Unlike most other Shi'ites, moreover, the Brethren never speak unfavorably of the first three caliphs of Islam, Abu Bakr (d. 634), 'Umar (d. 644), and 'Uthman (d. 656). They even hold up 'Uthman as a model of piety and resignation, along with great figures such as Socrates, Jesus, and Husayn, telling us that he ordered his slaves to put away their swords when they prepared to fight the men who had come to kill him (*R.* IV, 74-75). This is surprising, but the Brethren regarded "disavowal, vilification, calumniation, and cursing" as a disagreeable aspect of popular Shi'ism, as we have seen, and they praise the

Prophet for having refused to curse his fellow-tribesmen when they fought against them; instead, he asked God to guide them because they did not know what they were doing, invoking Noah, who had done the same. Far from cursing 'Uthman and other figures hated by the Shi'ites, one should accept the will of God and resign oneself to His predetermined decree. It is not for nothing that the Brethren have acquired a reputation for tolerance.

IMAGINED PROPAGANDA

Given the eirenic outlook of the Brethren, how did they go about trying to recruit adherents for their brotherhood? They answer this question by describing themselves as leaders of a major propaganda network, studding their encyclopaedia with instructions to their brother-reader on ways in which they should find, recognize, select, persuade, and eventually win the hearts and the minds of potential adherents to the cause. In most cases, they warn their potential missionaries of the danger that secrets may be disclosed to people outside the brotherhood or even that spies may be acting for opponents of the doctrine. These warnings were all the more necessary because the spread of the message took the form, according to the Brethren, of a healing destined to penetrate all ranks of society. They make big claims for their own influence.

On two occasions in Epistle 48 we find a passage specifying where adherents have already been recruited and how the recruitment of new members is to be effected. The passage is worth quoting at some length, for it gives a good idea of how extensive and elaborate the whole system of propaganda was supposed to be:

> We have brethren and friends among noble and virtuous people in (various) countries. Some of them are the children of kings, governors, ministers, officials and secretaries, others of noblemen, land-owners, traders and farmers, still others of scholars, litterateurs, jurists and bearers of the religion, while others are children of craftsmen, administrators and trustees of people. To each group we have delegated one of our brethren whose clear-sightedness

> and knowledge we have approved, to serve them as our substitute in advising them with kindness, mercy and solicitude ... We have chosen you, my merciful friend – May God stand by you, as well as by ourselves, with a spirit coming from Him! – so that you may help them, and we have approved you so that you may share with them the virtue which God has given to you in the form of intellect, understanding, discernment, courage of the soul, purity of its substance, and so that you may assist them and support your brethren, since your substance is part of their substances and your soul is part of their souls (*R.* IV, 165 and, with only trifling divergences, IV, 188).

So if the Brethren are to be believed, they had converts in practically every stratum of society. Indeed, they here describe themselves as endowed with a following so sizable that one would expect them to have been mentioned in the chronicles as leaders of a major religious movement. But this they were clearly not. What they are describing here seems to be complete fiction, or alternatively it is a description of the Ismaili mission, to which it applies with great precision. If so, the Brethren would here be treating Ismailism much as they treated Shi'ism in the passage above, namely, as their own private property, they, supposedly, being the true leaders of both. There is at all events no question of treating this as an accurate account of their own network.

The Brethren also describe themselves as keen propagandists in the concluding part of the "Table of Contents" (*Fihrist*), at the very beginning of the encyclopaedia, in which they stress the importance of only addressing suitable candidates:

> This is how things should be also for whoever is in possession of these epistles and the "(Comprehensive) Epistle." The owner should not damage them by leaving them in the hands of unsuitable people or by giving them to people who have no desire for them, nor should he fail to do them justice by withholding them from persons worthy of them or by turning them away from someone who deserves them. He should communicate them only to those who are free, good, right, clear-sighted in their aspiration, and supportive of right guidance, from among the seekers of knowledge, cultivators of literature,

> and lovers of wisdom. May he take the greatest care in the way he preserves, conceals, discloses and reveals the epistles, may he protect them with the greatest of protections, and may he safeguard them with the best of safeguards! (*R.* I, 44-45).

The Brethren of Purity thus come across as masters of propaganda, thoroughly convinced of their mission and their ability to carry it out, endowed with a seemingly infallible method of recruiting new adherents, a well-organized system for taking care of them, and last but not least, a sound program of ethical and intellectual education for their instruction. Taken at face value, all this would suggest that their intention was to lead a powerful movement designed to resist, oppose, and eventually overthrow the current religious (and perhaps even political) establishment. But this is most unlikely. For in the entire corpus of epistles one can hardly find a single passage in which such an intention is discernible. On the contrary, the impression one gets throughout is that the authors were too busy with philosophical abstractions to play any sort of active role on the political scene. In fact, we need only remind ourselves of the Sleepers in the Cave to realize what the genuine attitude of our Brethren may have been, since it is with them that they most readily wished to be identified. Sleeping until better days had come and trying to predict from the stars when this would happen: these were not the most obvious ways to lead a religious and/or political revolution!

THE SESSIONS OF SCIENCE

In practice, one would assume that the Brethren only recruited adherents among people they met in Basra and unknown readers of their epistles, who may have set out to share their convictions with others at times. At all events, in Basra they held regular meetings which they call "sessions of science" (*majalis al-'ilm*) and which they urge their readers to replicate wherever they may live. These meetings are mentioned with some frequency in the *Rasa'il*, as in the passage at the head of this chapter. On several occasions they are connected with the theme of the four "ultimate books" discussed at the end of Chapter 5, suggesting that they served to provide new members of the brotherhood with the opportunity to be initiated and closely supervised by more accomplished followers of the doctrine, much as in modern freemasonry and, perhaps, in the ancient Pythagorean schools. We have every reason to believe that the program of these sessions was fundamentally similar, if not absolutely identical, to the one still perceptible through the arrangement of the Epistles. The beginning of Epistle 45 informs us that brethren should have such meetings wherever they lived and that they should meet at fixed times, with nobody apart from themselves being allowed to attend, in order to discuss their sciences and their secrets. More precisely, the discussion should deal with the science of the soul, the sense and the sensible, the intellect and the intelligible as well as the study of the divine books, the prophetic revelations, and the meaning of what the divine law ordains. They should be concerned with the four mathematical sciences as well, but above all they should be devoted to the divine sciences, since these were the sciences which constituted the supreme aim of all sessions (*R.* IV, 41).

In a passage from the "Comprehensive Epistle" (*J.*, II, 395), it is suggested that the Brethren's sessions of science take place every twelve days. Netton compares this indication with what we know of certain Ismaili meetings during the Fatimid period in Egypt, namely that these "were held twice a week on Mondays and Thursdays for textual reading and study" (Netton, 2002: 3). But in addition to being rather far-fetched, it is very doubtful whether this kind of comparison may help us to situate our Brethren better in the large spectrum of secret societies known to have existed in tenth-century Islam.

METAPHORS FOR UTOPIA

The Brethren's penchant for abstract and idealistic schemes has been stressed on several occasions. I should like to conclude the present chapter by adducing two further examples which I view as especially illustrative of that tendency. The first is about the "Virtuous and Spiritual City" (*al-madina al-fadila al-'aqliyya*) which the Ikhwan invite their noble brethren to build together with them. This theme is referred to in various epistles, but I think the following extract, which also comes from Epistle 48, will suffice to illustrate the point:

> The construction of that City should be in the kingdom of the great Legislator, Who reigns over the souls and the bodies, since whoever reigns over the souls reigns over the bodies too, and whoever does not reign over the souls does not reign over the bodies either. The inhabitants of this City should form a people of the best, wise, and virtuous men endowed with insight into the affairs of the souls and their states, and thus into the affairs of the bodies and their states as well. The inhabitants of this City should adhere to a beautiful, noble and good conduct in their dealings with one another, and to another conduct in their dealings with the inhabitants of unjust cities. This City should not be built on the earth, where the tempers of the inhabitants of all the unjust cities are. Nor should it be built on the surface of water, since it would be hit by the waves and the troubles by which people who live in coastal cities are afflicted; nor should this city be built high in the air, lest the smoke of the unjust cities ascend to it and its airs become troubled. It is fitting that it should overlook other cities, so that its inhabitants can observe the states of the inhabitants of other cities at all times. And it should be based on the fear of God so that its buildings will not collapse. Its edifice should be erected on truthfulness in (public) utterances and assent in (private) consciences, while its pillars should be completed with loyalty and fidelity so that it will last and its perfection will be in agreement with the objective of the ultimate aim, that is, eternal life in felicity (*R.* IV, 171–172).

This hardly sounds realistic. A city that should be built neither on earth nor on water, but which should overlook all other cities and which should be based on fear of God, truthfulness, and fidelity: all this suggests some kind of heavenly city. On top of that, the Brethren's City is one based on a hierarchy of four classes of citizens, the craftsmen, the leaders, the kings, and the "divine men." Add that the City's four walls are said to be made of people's ignorance and you will take the Spiritual City of the Brethren for what it is, namely yet another of those literary fictions so much in favor with our authors and which may be compared with Plato's or Farabi's theories of the ideal constitution.

After building this metaphorical City the Brethren promise to "build the vessel who is the Ship of Salvation, in such a way that the Ship is loaded with the weight of the bodies and the City becomes the shelter of the spirits" (*R.* IV, 172). Apparently, the saving role of the ship lies in its removal service. Here, as in the case of the Cave and the City, the Brethren have appropriated an old theme – in this particular case the biblical story of Noah's Ark (to which there is an explicit reference in Epistle 44) and adapted it to their own purposes.

The way the Brethren take up, transform and intertwine themes as rich and symbolically expressive as the Ark, the Cave, or the Spiritual City is clear evidence of their extreme ability in that field. But however varied and suggestive the metaphors, the message remains essentially the same. It could be summarized as the necessity to preserve science in all its aspects, how adverse and painful the circumstances of this world might be, and the conviction that this alone enabled man to reach the world of eternal felicity. The message need not be new. On the contrary, the sheer age of the message vouchsafed its authenticity, as the Brethren themselves say: "ours is not a modern opinion or an invented sect, but the old opinion followed in all times by philosophers, sages, prophets, caliphs and imams: it is the religion of Abraham" (*R.* IV, 126). All thinking men had adhered to the same unchanging truth since the human discovery of monotheism, conventionally credited to Abraham. One just had to make sure that it continued to be transmitted.

EPILOGUE

One millennium later, one cannot help being impressed by the way in which the Brethren's ship managed to get round the reefs of time. Manuscripts of the Epistles are found by the dozen in many parts of the world. Some of them are magnificently illuminated, such as the copy completed by Hasan b. al-Nu'mani al-Isma'ili in the sixteenth century, now part of the collection of the Institute of Ismaili Studies in London. Others, like the Istanbul manuscript Atif Efendi 1681, date to the end of the twelfth or the beginning of the thirteenth centuries, that is to say from the period when the *Rasa'il* seem to have first been claimed by the Tayyibi branch. It may well be that most of the illustrated manuscripts are Ismaili, but many must have been copied for Sunnis or Imami Shi'ites.

The profusion of manuscripts is surprising, for there was much hostility to them among Sunnis for their Shi'ism and their philosophy alike. The tenth-century Mu'tazilite theologian 'Abd al-Jabbar was virulently hostile, as we saw in the first pages of this book. The Abbasid caliph Mustanjid (r. 1160–1170) had the Epistles publicly burnt in Baghdad about 1160 along with Ibn Sina's famous "Healing" (*Shifa'*). The Brethren's book was "wholly heresy and reviling of Islam; it should not be read or studied, but must be burnt," as a mirror for princes composed around the middle of the twelfth century declared. Even philosophically inclined people might disapprove of them. To Abu Sulayman al-Mantiqi (d. c. 985), their attempt to combine Arabic legislation with Greek philosophy was fundamentally mistaken, as we saw in Chapter 1. To Ghazali (d. 1111), a theologian who might have been expected to condemn them on grounds of heresy, their main weakness was rather that they followed Pythagoras, a "weak philosopher" criticized already by Aristotle.

For all that, one would assume the Epistles to have been on the reading list of most members of the educated upper class endowed with an interest in philosophy and science, whether they found them to be weak or not. Thus Ibn Sina's father, a member of the bureaucracy in eastern Iran, had studied them, as had Ibn Sina himself. The father was Ismaili, but the chances are that he read the *Rasa'il* because he was a highly educated professional man (working as a secretary in the local bureaucracy) rather than because he was Ismaili. The son was not Ismaili, but it appears that the Brethren's work had exerted a significant influence on him in his youth. The polymath Biruni (d. after 1050) had also read them, though he did not think much of them, and so had other scientists. As Susanne Diwald observes, entire passages from the Epistles appear almost word for word in works by Idrisi (d. 1165), the renowned geographer and botanist, and in the *Cosmography* of Qazwini (d. 1283). There were even traditionalists who liked them. A member of the Hanbali legal school (and grandson of the famous mystic 'Abd al-Qadir al-Jilani), who died in 1214, had all his books thrown to the fire: the Epistles of the Brethren were among them. And Ibn Taymiyya (d. 1328), a reformer from the same school, held that the Epistles had merits, despite their theological errors.

On the whole, their readership seems to have been philosophically low-brow by Avicennian standards, that is, more inclined to spirituality, mysticism, and their own inner lives than the mechanics of the world around them. They included an Imami Shi'ite such as Ibn Ta'us (d. 1266), an ascetically-inclined person whose interest in philosophy seems to have been limited to ethics, and Suhrawardi (d. 1191), the "Shaykh of Illuminism." Diwald, who noted the Brethren's influence on Suhrawardi, could also have cited a number of his heirs, from Shahrazuri in the thirteenth century up to Mulla Sadra Shirazi, the famous Iranian philosopher and mystic who died around 1640. As yet, scholarship has only begun to take account of the influence exerted by the Brethren on these and other great Iranian thinkers who sought, like the Brethren themselves, to connect philosophical reflections with techniques of inner purification as practiced by the Sufis.

Needless to say, Islamic mysticism as such offers another large field to prospect. The way was paved by Louis Massignon, who in his *Recueil de textes inédits concernant l'histoire de la mystique en pays d'Islam* stressed the impact of our *Rasa'il* on figures as emblematic as al-Ghazali in his "Revivification of the [religious] Sciences" and Ibn al-'Arabi (d. 1241) in his "Revelations of Mekka." The case of al-Ghazali may be seen as typical of the level of hypocrisy an author may reach when it comes to acknowledgment of sources, for though he dismissed the work of the Brethren, he adopted a number of their views without acknowledgment. Particularly illustrative is the way in which his *Risalat al-laduniyya* is modeled on, or at least inspired by, the general classification of sciences adopted by the Brethren in Epistle 7. It may be added in passing that the Yemeni ruler and litterateur Malik al-Afdal (d. 1377) similarly used their classification of sciences without acknowledgment in his mirror for princes, while telling us that the Epistles mix falsehood with truth to trap those of weak intellects. Apparently, it was in order for the intellectually strong to plunder the *Rasa'il* for the truths in question.

Leaving the East, we turn our attention to the impact of the Epistles in the West. According to the "Generations of Nations" (*Tabaqat al-umam*) written in the eleventh century by the Toledan Sa'id al-Andalusi, the *Rasa'il Ikhwan al-Safa'* were introduced into Spain by a man named Kirmani. The crucial passage reads:

> Kirmani, from Cordoba, was one of those who had a thorough knowledge of arithmetic and geometry. His pupil, the geometer and arithmetician Ibn Hayy, told me that he had never met anyone able to compete with his master in geometry or to emulate him in solving the intricacies of that science, in explaining its problems or offering an exhaustive treatment of its parts. Kirmani had travelled to the East and reached Harran in the Jazira [i.e., High-Mesopotamia]. There he had dealt with geometry and medicine. He then came back to Al-Andalus [i.e., Spain] and settled in the West, in the city of Zaragoza, bringing with him the work known as the *Epistles of the Brethren of Purity*. To the best of my knowledge, no-one had introduced them into Al-Andalus before him (*Tabaqat*, ed. Cheikho, pp. 70-71).

From what comes next in Sa'id's statement we learn that Kirmani died in Zaragoza in AH 458 (1066 CE), at about ninety years of age, which indicates that the *Rasa'il* were probably known in Spain by the middle of the eleventh century. This, as may be noted, coincides with the time of writing of the "Aim of the Sage" (*Ghayat al-Hakim*), the highly influential treatise on magic and other occult sciences which we encountered in Chapter 1. The precise authorship of this work remains a problem, but we may be certain that it was written in Spain. In fact, whereas Ibn Khaldun and others identify the author of the treatise as the well-known astronomer and mathematician Maslama al-Majriti, who died shortly after 1000 CE, internal evidence leads one rather to assume that the book was written towards the middle of the eleventh century and it is, therefore, customary to refer to its author, who cannot otherwise be identified, as Pseudo-Majriti. The reason why all this is worth bringing up again is twofold. First, it may be recalled here that Pseudo-Majriti alludes to a set of *rasa'il* he had composed, and that this was understood as a reference to our Epistles. Second, whether this identification is correct or not it appears that the *Ghayat al-Hakim* was significantly influenced by our Epistles. Once again, the nature of the topic forces us to consider the possibility of various channels of transmission, including oral ones, acting at the same time, so that it proves difficult at times to distinguish between what comes from the *Rasa'il* and what from, say, the innumerable works on alchemy ascribed to Jabir b. Hayyan (d. c. 815). But that the *Rasa'il* contributed is not open to doubt. Martin Plessner has noted many verbal echoes of our Epistles in the *Ghaya*, some extending over several pages. Indeed, the overall influence of the Epistles on the *Ghaya* could go well beyond textual borrowings. It may have been the general affinity between the two works rather than mere coincidence that led some to believe Maslama al-Majriti to have written the Epistles, or at least the "Comprehensive Epistle," himself.

The enormous success that the *Ghayat al-Hakim* was to have in turn in Europe until the Renaissance leads us to consider the indirect influence that the *Rasa'il Ikhwan al-Safa'* may have exerted there. Unlike other Arabic works available in Spain in the twelfth and thirteenth centuries, it does not seem that the Epistles were translated in full into Latin, although we know that some of them – most notably Epistle 4 (on geography), Epistle 14 (on the Posterior Analytics), and parts of Epistle 52 (on magic) – did make their way to the

Latin world. But the *Ghayat al-Hakim* was certainly translated and it became hugely influential in Latin translation, or rather adaptation, in which it was known as the *Picatrix*. Many other works translated into Latin might have relayed a phrase, an idea, or a theory originally penned in Arabic by the Brethren. Thus the famous *Secreta Secretorum* (Arabic *Sirr al-asrar*), a treatise of advice on government and sundry other things attributed to Aristotle, contains several passages from the *Rasa'il*. Even the translated parts of the *Shifa'*, Ibn Sina's *magnum opus* in philosophy, might be worth examining from this point of view, if only because his way of classifying the philosophical sciences much resembles that elaborated by the Brethren.

One must surely also remember that a number of major medieval Jewish thinkers, such as Ibn Paquda and Ibn Gabirol in the eleventh century, and Moses Ibn Ezra and Maimonides in the twelfth century, were Neoplatonists whose mysticism and asceticism have been shown to be indebted to the Ikhwanian corpus. The impact of our encyclopaedists on the Jewish–Arabic milieu of al-Andalus is another theme likely to yield interesting discoveries, as would perhaps the fainter echo of the Epistles that reverberated in the Latin West.

GUIDE TO FURTHER READING

EDITIONS AND TRANSLATIONS

Pending the completion of a new edition (with English translation) of the corpus of epistles as a whole, those who wish to read the Arabic original must use one of the three imperfect editions of the work, made in Bombay (1888, in four volumes), Cairo (ed. Khayr al-Din Zirikli, 1928, in four volumes), and Beirut (ed. B. al-Bustani, Dar Sadir, 1957, in four volumes). It is the Beirut edition which has been used here. For the *Risalat-al-Jami'a*, I have used the edition by J. Saliba (Damascus, 1949, in two volumes). Readers who only have access to the Bombay or Cairo editions can easily convert the references given by means of D. R.Blumenthal's, "A Comparative Table of Bombay, Cairo and Beirut Editions of the *Rasa'il Ikhwan al-Safa*'", in *Arabica*, 21 (1974), 186–203.

As mentioned above, there is no complete modern translation of the *Rasa'il*, but there are translations of individual epistles (or groups of epistles) in a number of Western languages. For the long parable of the debate between men and animals (Epistle 22), see L. E. Goodman, *The Case of the Animals versus Man before the King of the Jinn. A Tenth-Century Ecological Fable of the Pure Brethren of Basra* (Boston, 1978). This translation is designed for the general reader and is easily accessible. S. Diwald, *Arabische Philosophie und Wissenschaft in der Enzyklopädie.* Kitâb Ikhwân as-Safâ' *(III) Die Lehre von Seele und Intellekt* (Wiesbaden, 1975), provides a German translation of Epistles 32 to 41. This is a highly useful study for the scholar, but it is not suitable for the beginner. The reader may benefit more from C. Baffioni, *L'Epistola degli Ikhwân al-Safâ' "Sulle Opinioni e le Religioni"* (Naples, 1989) and G. de Callataÿ, *Ikhwân al-Safâ'. Les Révolutions et les cycles* (Louvain-la-Neuve–Beirut, 1996), since these translations (of Epistles 42 and 36 respectively) are both accompanied by a substantial introduction and an extensive range of notes. Most of the other translations published so far are found only in scholarly periodicals and do not seem appropriate for the beginner. A short but useful summary of all epistles has been given in Italian by A. Bausani, *L'Enciclopedia dei Fratelli della Purità. Riassunto, con introduzione e breve commento, dei 52 Trattati o Epistole degli Ikhwân al-Safâ'* (Naples, 1978).

DISCUSSION

For the historical and doctrinal background, the reader is advised to consult the following recent studies.

Corbin, H. *History of Islamic Philosophy*. London, 1993

Crone, P. *Medieval Islamic Political Thought*. Edinburgh, 2004 (parts III and IV)

Daftari, F. *The Ismailis: Their History and Doctrines*. Cambridge, 1990

Gutas, D. *Greek Thought, Arabic Culture. The Graeco-Arabic Translation Movement in Baghdad and Early 'Abbasid Society (2nd–4th / 8th–10th c.)*. London, 1998

Halm, H. *Shiism*. Edinburgh, 1994

Kraemer, J. L. *Humanism in the Renaissance of Islam: The Cultural Revival during the Buyid Age*. Leiden, 1992

For a general introduction to the Ikhwan's thought, the lay reader may start with I. R. Netton, *Muslim Neoplatonists. An Introduction to the Thought of the Brethren of Purity (Ikhwân al-Safâ')* (London, 2002, reprinted from 1982), an easy survey which concentrates on different aspects of the Epistles from the present work. Other easily accessible (but older) materials are the articles "Ikhwân al-Safâ'" by Y. Marquet, in *Dictionary of Scientific Biography*, XV, Suppl. I (New York, 1978), pp. 249–251, and in *Encyclopaedia of Islam*, new edition, III, pp. 1071–1076.

Readers wishing to read more deeply into the subject may find the following useful.

Marquet, Y. *La philosophie des Ikhwân al-Safâ'. Thèse présentée devant l'Université de Paris IV, le 12 juin 1971*. Algiers, 1973. A learned work, often referred to in this book, but not free of prejudice. A revised, yet substantially unchanged, version of this book was published in 1999 (Paris-Milan).

Baffioni, C. *Frammenti e testimonianze di autori antichi nelle epistole degli Ikhwân al-Safâ'*. Rome, 1994. Another valuable contribution, especially for the question of sources.

On more individual aspects of the Ikhwan and their Epistles, see the following selection of works, all of them mentioned or referred to in this book.

Casanova, P. "Une Date astronomique dans les Epîtres des Ikhwân as-Safâ'". *Journal Asiatique*, series XI, V (1915), 5–17

de Callataÿ, G. *Annus platonicus. A Study of World Cycles in Greek, Latin and Arabic Sources*. Louvain-la-Neuve, 1996

—— "Sacredness and Esotericism in the *Rasâ'il Ikhwân al-Safâ'*". In D. De Smet, G. de Callataÿ and J. M. F. Van Reeth (eds), *Al-Kitâb. La sacralité du texte dans le monde de l'Islam*. Actes du Symposium International tenu à Leuven et Louvain-la-Neuve du 29 mai au 1 juin 2002, Brussels–Louvain-la-Neuve–Leuven, 2004, pp. 389–401

—— "Astrology and prophecy: The Ikhwân al-Safâ' and the Legend of the Seven Sleepers". In Ch. Burnett, J. P. Hogendijk, K. Plofker, and M. Yano (eds), *Studies in the History of the Exact Sciences in Honour of David Pingree*, Leiden–Boston (2004), pp. 758–785

Goldziher, I. "Über die Benennung der Ikhwân as-Safâ'". *Der Islam*, I (1910), pp. 22–26

Hamdâni, A. "The Arrangement of the *Rasâ'il Ikhwân al-Safâ'* and the Problem of Interpolations". *Journal of Semitic Studies*, XXIX (1984), pp. 97–110

Lane-Poole, S. *The Brotherhood of Purity*. Lahore, 1960

Marquet, Y. "Imâmat, résurrection et hiérarchie selon les Ikhwân al-Safâ'". *Revue des Études Islamiques*, XXX (1962), pp. 49–142

—— "Sabéens et Ikhwân al-Safâ'". *Studia Islamica*, XXIV (1966), pp. 35-80 and XXV (1966), pp. 77–109

—— "La détermination astrale de l'évolution selon les Frères de la Pureté". *Bulletin d'Etudes Orientales*, XLIV (1992), pp. 127–146

Massignon, L. *Recueil de textes inédits concernant l'histoire de la mystique en pays d'Islam*. Paris, 1929

Nasr, S. H. *An Introduction to Islamic Cosmological Doctrines. Conceptions of Nature and Methods used for its Study by the Ikhwân al-Safâ', al-Bîrûnî, and Ibn Sînâ*. Cambridge, Mass., 1964, pp. 23–104

Netton, I. R. "Brotherhood versus Imâmate: Ikhwân al-Safâ' and the Ismâ'îlis". *Jerusalem Studies in Arabic and Islam*, II (1980), pp. 253–262

Pinès, Sh. "Une encyclopédie arabe du 10e siècle, *Les Épîtres des Frères de la Pureté, Rasâ'il Ikhwân al-Safâ'* ". *Rivista di storia della filosofia*, XL (1985), pp. 131–136

Pingree, D. "Some of the Sources of the *Ghâyat al-Hakîm*". *Journal of the Warburg and Courtauld Institutes*, XLIII (1980), pp. 1–15

Plessner, M. M. "Beiträge zur islamischen Literaturgeschichte IV: Samuel Miklos Stern, die Ikhwân al-Safâ' und die *Encyclopaedia of Islam*". *Israel Oriental Studies*, II (1972), pp. 353–361

Stern, S. "The Authorship of the Epistles of the Ikhwân as-Safâ'". *Islamic Culture* (Hyderabad), XX (1946), pp. 367–372

—— "New Information about the Authors of the 'Epistles of the Sincere Brethren'". *Islamic Studies* (Karachi), III (1964), pp. 405–428; reprinted in idem, *Studies in Early Ismâ'îlism*. Leiden, 1983, pp. 155–176

INDEX OF PASSAGES FROM THE *RASA'IL IKHWAN AL-SAFA'*

References are made to the Beirut edition (ed. B. al-Bustani, Dar Sadir, 1957, in four volumes) for the *Rasa'il* and to the edition by J. Saliba (Damascus, 1949, in two volumes) for the *Risalat-al-Jami'a*.

GENERAL INDEX

MAKERS *of the* MUSLIM WORLD

Series Editor: Patricia Crone
Institute for Advanced Study, Princeton

Among the over fifty titles in the series:

Ibn 'Arabi
William C. Chittick
Renowned expert William Chittick surveys the life and works of this legendary thinker.
ISBN: 1-85168-387-9

Shaykh Mufid
T. Bayhom-Daou
An assessment of the great Shi'ite scholar and theologian.
ISBN: 1-85168-383-6

Abu Nuwas
Philip Kennedy
A readable introduction to this celebrated 9th-century poet.
ISBN: 1-85168-360-7

'Abd al-Malik
Chase F. Robinson
The Umayyad Caliph and founder of the Dome of the Rock is captured in a concise and clear manner.
ISBN: 1-85168-361-5

Fazlallah Astarabadi and the Hurufis
Shahzad Bashir
Discusses the achievements of this Sufi thinker and founder of Gnostic Hurufism.
ISBN: 1-85168-385-2

al-Ma'mun
Michael Cooperson
An introduction to the controversial 9th-century Caliph and patron of the sciences.
ISBN: 1-85168-386-0

Ahmad Riza Khan
Usha Sanyal
On the founder of the 'Barelwi' movement in India in the late 19th/early 20th centuries.
ISBN: 1-85168-359-3

Amir Khusraw
Sunil Sharma
Surveys the life and work of the 14th-century Indian poet, courtier, musician, and Sufi.
ISBN: 1-85168-362-3

'Abd al-Rahman III
Maribel Fierro
Introduces the founder of the great Caliphate of Madinat al-Zahra at Cordova.
ISBN: 1-85168-384-4

el-Hajj Beshir Agha
Jane Hathaway
An examination of the longest serving Chief Harem Eunuch in the history of the Ottoman Empire.
ISBN: 1-85168-390-9